Terrorism: Section by Section Analysis of the USA PATRIOT Act

Summary

The Uniting and Strengthening America by Providing Appropriate Tools Required to Intercept and Obstruct Terrorism (USA PATRIOT) Act, P. L. 107-56, is part of the Congressional response to September 11. It is the merger of two similar bills. S.1510 passed the Senate on October 11, 147 *Cong.Rec.* S10604, and H.R.2975 passed the House on October 12 after substituting the language of H.R.3108 for its text, 147 *Cong.Rec.* H6775. Having informally resolved their differences, the House enacted the measure in final form on October 24, 147 *Cong.Rec.* H7282, and the Senate on October 25, 147 *Cong.Rec.* S11059.

The Act consists of ten titles which, among other things:

• give federal law enforcement and intelligence officers greater authority (at least temporarily) to gather and share evidence particularly with respect to wire and electronic communications;

• amend federal money laundering laws, particularly those involving overseas financial activities;

• create new federal crimes, increase the penalties for existing federal crimes, and adjust existing federal criminal procedure, particularly with respect to acts of terrorism;

• modify immigration law, increasing the ability of federal authorities to prevent foreign terrorists from entering the U.S., to detain foreign terrorist suspects, to deport foreign terrorists, and to mitigate the adverse immigration consequences for the foreign victims of September 11; and

• authorize appropriations to enhance the capacity of immigration, law enforcement, and intelligence agencies to more effectively respond to the threats of terrorism.

Several proposals, offered while the Act was under consideration, were not among the provisions ultimately enacted, *e.g.*, revision of the McDade-Murtha Amendment (relating to the application of professional conduct standards to federal prosecutors), measures to combat illegal Internet gambling, and are thus beyond the scope of this report.

Contents

Terrorism: Section by Section Analysis of the USA PATRIOT Act

Introduction

The Uniting and Strengthening America by Providing Appropriate Tools Required to Intercept and Obstruct Terrorism (USA PATRIOT) Act, Public Law 107-56, is part of the Congressional response to September 11. It is the merger of two similar bills. S.1510 passed the Senate on October 11, 147 *Cong.Rec.* S10604, and H.R.2975 passed the House on October 12 after substituting the language of H.R.3108 for its text, 147 *Cong.Rec.* H6775. Having informally resolving their differences, the House enacted the measure in final form on October 24, 147 *Cong.Rec.* H7282, and the Senate on October 25, 147 *Cong.Rec.* S11059.

The report of the House Committee on the Judiciary, H.Rept. 107-236 on H.R.2975, and the report of the House Committee on Financial Services, H.Rept. 107-250 on H.R. 3004, each explain some of the issues ultimately resolved in the Act.

This is a section by section analysis of the Act as enacted. The analysis borrows the explanations of the House Committee of the Judiciary, in a number of those instances where the language of the Committee bill and the language of the Act are identical.

Section 1. Short Title and Table of Contents.

The Act may be cited as the "Uniting and Strengthening America by Providing Appropriate Tools Required to Intercept and Obstruct Terrorism (USA PATRIOT ACT) Act of 2001."

Section 2. Construction; Severability.

Section 2 confirms that the Act's provisions should be given maximum effect and that should any provision be found invalid or unenforceable it should be severed and the remainder the Act allowed to remain in effect.

Title I – Enhancing Domestic Security Against Terrorism

Section 101. Counterterrorism Fund.

Congress created a Counterterrorism Fund to reimburse the Department of Justice for the costs of reestablishing operating capacity lost as a consequence of the destruction of the Alfred P. Murrah Federal Building in Oklahoma City and for other counterterrorism expenditures, Public Law 104-19, 109 Stat. 249 (1995). This section takes a similar course in order to reimburse the Justice Department for the costs of (1) reestablishing the operating capacity of facilities damaged or destroyed by terrorists; (2) preventing, investigating and prosecuting terrorism by various means including the payment of rewards (without limitation); and (3) conducting terrorism threat assessments of federal facilities. The Fund is also available to reimburse federal agencies for costs associated with overseas detention of individuals accused of terrorism in violation of United States law.

Section 102. Sense of Congress Condemning Discrimination Against Arab and Muslim Americans.

It is the sense of Congress that the civil rights and civil liberties of all Americans, including Arab Americans, Muslim Americans, and Americans from South Asia, should be protected; that violence and discrimination against any American should be condemned; and that the patriotism of Americans from every ethnic, racial, and religious background should be acknowledged.

Section 103. Increased Funding for the Technical Support Center at the Federal Bureau of Investigation.

This section authorizes appropriations of $200 million for each of fiscal years 2002, 2003, and 2004 for the FBI's Technical Support Center, created by section 811 of the Antiterrorism and Effective Death Penalty Act of 1996 (Public Law 104-132, 110 Stat. 1314 (1996).

Section 104. Requests for Military Assistance to Enforce Prohibition in Certain Emergencies.

The Posse Comitatus Act and its administrative auxiliaries, 18 U.S.C. 1385, 10 U.S.C. 375, ban the use of the armed forces to execute civilian law, absent explicit statutory permission. Pre-existing statutory exceptions covered Department of Justice requests for technical assistance in connection with emergencies involving biological, chemical or nuclear weapons, 18 U.S.C. 2332e, 175a, 229E, 831(e), and 10 U.S.C. 382. This section amends section 2332e to include emergencies involving other weapons of mass destruction.

Section 105. Expansion of National Electronic Crime Task Force Initiative.

In order to counter various forms of electronic crime including those directed against the Nation's critical infrastructure and financial systems, this section instructs the Director of the United States Secret Service to establish a network of electronic crime task forces modeled after the New York Electronic Crimes Task Force.

Section 106. Presidential Authority.

The International Emergency Economic Powers Act (IEEPA), 50 U.S.C. 1701 *et seq.*, grants the President emergency economic powers when faced with extraordinary threats to our national security, foreign policy or economic well being. Under such conditions, for example, he may freeze the assets located in this country of a foreign nation or national responsible for the threat. During war time, the Trading with the Enemy Act (TWEA) gives him the power to confiscate enemy property located in the United States , 50 U.S.C. App. 1 *et seq.*

Section 106 amends section 703 of IEEPA, 50 U.S.C. 1702, to permit the President to confiscate foreign property in response to foreign aggression. The authority becomes available when the United States is engaged in armed hostilities or has been attacked by a foreign country or its nationals. At that time, the property of any foreign person, organization, or nation which planned, authorized, aided or engaged in the hostilities or attack becomes forfeitable. The President or his delegate may determine the particulars under which the property is confiscated, administered and disposed of, subject to an innocent owner defense created by section 316 of the USA PATRIOT Act. Elsewhere, the USA PATRIOT Act gives the President an alternative means to confiscate the same property on similar grounds (section 806).

Section 106 is intriguing because on one hand it seems a logical extension of IEEPA and TWEA, but on the other it appears to revive the constitutionally suspect forfeiture of estate. Forfeiture of estate was a creature of the common law.[1] Upon conviction and attainder, a felon or traitor forfeited all of his property. Statutory forfeiture, a more familiar feature of American law, consists of the confiscation of contraband, the fruits of crimes, and the means to commit a crime – untaxed whiskey, the drug dealer's profits, and the rum runner's ship.

Three distinguishing features characterize forfeiture of estate. The property is lost solely by reason of its ownership by the felon or traitor; there need be no other nexus to the crime. As a consequence, it works the confiscation of all of a felon's property, not just his crime-related property. Third, it extinguishes his future right to hold property and no title to property may pass through him to his heirs.[2]

It is this last feature, this "corruption of the blood", which the authors of the Constitution found most distasteful. They decreed that "no attainder of treason shall work corruption of blood, or forfeiture except during the life of the person attainted," *U.S.Const.* Art. III, §3, cl.2. And when first assembled in Congress, they extended the ban to all federal crimes: "no conviction or judgment for any offences aforesaid, shall work corruption of blood, or any forfeiture of estate," 1 Stat. 117 (1790).[3]

---

[1] "Three kinds of forfeiture were established in England at the time the Eighth Amendment was ratified in the United States: deodand, forfeiture, and statutory forfeiture. . . . Of England's three kinds of forfeiture, only the third took hold in the United States," *Austin v. United States*, 509 U.S. 602, 611-12 (1993).

[2] Statutory forfeitures have often been accomplished through civil proceedings conducted *in rem* with the offending property treated as defendant. As a result, some came to believe that the necessity of the property owner's criminal conviction constituted the essential distinction between forfeiture of estate and statutory forfeiture. Yet, occasional forfeiture statutes have predicated confiscation upon the owner's conviction throughout our history. Moreover, it defies credibility to claim that forfeiture of estate's only ameliorating attribute is its only essential element.

[3] The statutory ban, and its successors, remained in effect until 1984 when it was repealed

(continued...)

During the Civil War, Congress authorized the confiscation of the property of supporters of the Confederacy, 12 Stat. 589 (1862), but in deference to President Lincoln's constitutional doubts interest in the property reverted to the offender's heirs upon his death, 12 Stat. 627 (1862).

On the other hand, confiscation under the Trading With the Enemy Act (TWEA), looks for all intents and purposes like the confiscation of estate of the property of an enemy nation or national, 50 U.S.C. App. 5(b). Yet the Supreme Court has upheld TWEA as a valid exercise of the war power without mentioning of any obstacle interposed by constitutional reservations concerning forfeiture of estate, *Silesian American Corp. v. Clark*, 332 U.S. 469 (1947).[4]

Section 106 also amends IEEPA to cover situations where either *the covered foreign person or* the covered property are within this country or otherwise subject to the jurisdiction of the United States. It allows the President to freeze assets during the pendency any International Emergency Economic Act investigation rather than await its outcome as was previously the case. Finally, it permits the government to present, in secret (*ex parte* and *in camera*), any classified information upon which an IEEPA decision has been based should the decision be subject to judicial review.

Title II – Enhanced Surveillance Procedures

Section 201. Authority to Intercept Wire, Oral, and Electronic Communications Relating to Terrorism.

Title III of the Omnibus Crime Control and Safe Streets Act of 1968, 18 U.S.C. 2510 *et seq.* establishes a judicially supervised procedure under which law enforcement authorities may intercept wire, oral, or electronic communications. The procedure, however, is only available in connection with the investigations of specifically designated serious crimes. Section 201 adds several terrorism offenses to Title III's list of designated offenses:

- chemical weapons offenses, 18 U.S.C. 229;
- use of weapons of mass destruction, 18 U.S.C. 2332a;
- violent acts of terrorism transcending national borders, 18 U.S.C. 2332b;
- financial transactions with countries which support terrorism, 18 U.S.C. 2332d;
- material support of terrorists, 18 U.S.C. 2339A; and

---

[3](...continued)
through misunderstanding as part of comprehensive revision of federal criminal law, 18 U.S.C. 3563 (1982 ed.).

[4] *Cf., Societe Internationale v. Rogers*, 357 U.S. 197, 211 (1958)("this summary power to seize property which is believed to be enemy-owned is rescued from constitutional invalidity under the Due Process and Just Compensation Clauses of the Fifth Amendment only by those provisions of the Act which afford a non-enemy claimant a later judicial hearing as to the propriety of the seizure")(no suggestion that due process likewise condemns forfeiture of estate in cases that do not involve treason).

! material support of terrorist organizations, 18 U.S.C. 2339B.

The section makes a technical correction in 18 U.S.C. 2516 by designating as 18 U.S.C. 2516(1)(r) one of the two paragraphs previously identified as 18 U.S.C. 2516(1)(p). Section 201 is subject to the sunset provisions of section 224.

Section 202. Authority to Intercept Wire, Oral, and Electronic Communications Relating to Computer Fraud and Abuse Offenses.

Section 202 adds computer fraud and abuse to the Title III predicate offense list. This section is subject to the sunset provisions of section 224.

Section 203. Authority to Share Criminal Investigative Information.

Previously, federal law enforcement officers who uncovered details of the activities of international terrorist organizations or of foreign agents in this country were often not free to pass the information on to federal intelligence officers. This section allows federal law enforcement officers to share a limited range of foreign intelligence information, notwithstanding earlier limitations such as those involving the use of grand jury information or Title III evidence.

Rule 6(e) of the Federal Rules of Criminal Procedure prohibits disclosure of matters occurring before a federal grand jury. The Rule recognizes exceptions for disclosures in other judicial proceedings, to prevent abuse of the grand jury process, for presentation of evidence to other grand juries, and to state law enforcement officials.

Section 203 creates an exception for intelligence matters. It covers information (1) related to the protection of the United States against a foreign attack or other foreign hostile action, against sabotage or international terrorism by a foreign power or its agents, or against foreign clandestine intelligence activities; (2) concerning a foreign power or territory related to the national defense, security, or foreign affairs activities of the United States; or (3) constituting foreign intelligence or counterintelligence as defined in section 3 of the National Security Act of 1947 (that is, (a) "information relating to the capabilities, intentions, or activities of foreign governments or elements thereof, foreign organizations, or foreign persons" or (b) "information gathered and activities conducted to protect against espionage, other intelligence activities, sabotage, or assassinations conducted by or on behalf of foreign governments or elements thereof, foreign organizations, or foreign persons," 50 U.S.C. 401a(2), (3)).

Now when such information comes to light during the course of a federal grand jury investigation, it may be passed on to other Federal law enforcement, intelligence, protective, immigration, national defense, or national security officials, but only for use in the official duties. Within a reasonable time thereafter, Federal prosecutors must notify the court of the disclosure under seal. Prosecutors must also follow disclosure procedures outlined by the Attorney General when sharing intelligence information that identifies an American citizen or a permanent resident alien.

When authorities executing a Title III interception order discover this same type of intelligence evidence, they may reveal it to any of these same officers for use in their official duties. Before the passage of section 203, such information could only be shared for law enforcement purposes, 18 U.S.C. 2517. As in the case of grand jury information, Title III intelligence information that identifies an American citizen or a permanent resident alien can be divulged only pursuant to disclosure procedures outlined by the Attorney General.

Finally, section 203 creates a generic exception to any other law which purports to bar federal law enforcement officials from disclosing this type of intelligence information to these federal officers for official use. The section's amendments to Title III are subject to the sunset provisions of section 224, the grand jury and generic exceptions are not.

Section 204. Clarification of Intelligence Exceptions From Limitations on Interception and Disclosure of Wire, Oral and Electronic Communications.

Title III at one time stated that the interception of wire or oral communications for foreign intelligence purposes should be governed by the provisions of the Foreign Intelligence Surveillance Act (FISA) rather than those of Title III or of chapter 121 of title 18 of the United States Code (relating to stored wire and electronic communications and transactional records access) or of the Federal Communications Act, 18 U.S.C. 2511(2)(f). Section 204 amends this instruction in 18 U.S.C. 2511(2)(f) to confirm that in foreign intelligence investigations, FISA governs the interception of electronic communications and the use of pen registers and trap and trace devices as well. This section is subject to the sunset provisions of section 224.

Section 205. Employment of Translators by the Federal Bureau of Investigation.

Existing law sometimes waives personnel requirements and limitations in order to fill positions requiring foreign language skills, *e.g.*, 22 U.S.C. 1474(1)(relating to employment of translators with respect to United States Information and Educational Exchange Programs); 22 U.S.C. 4024(a)(4)(B) (relating to the employment of linguists in connection United States Foreign Service training).

Section 205 waives otherwise applicable personnel requirements and limitations to permit the Federal Bureau of Investigation (FBI) to hire translators expeditiously to support counterintelligence investigations and operations. The Director of the FBI will see to the necessary security requirements. The Attorney General will report to the Committees on the Judiciary on the number of translators employed by the FBI and by the Department of Justice, on the impediments to using translators employed by other government agencies, on the FBI's needs, and on his recommendations to meet the FBI's needs for translation services. This section is not subject to the sunset provisions of section 224.

Section 206. Roving Surveillance Authority Under the Foreign Intelligence Surveillance Act of 1978.

Speaking of identical language in an earlier bill, the House Committee on the Judiciary explained: "Section 1805(c)(2)(B) of title 50, permits the FISA court to order third parties, like common carriers, custodians, landlords and others, who are specified in the order, (specified persons) to provide assistance and information to law enforcement authorities in the installation of a wiretap or the collection of information related to a foreign intelligence investigation.

"Section 152 amends 1805(c)(2)(B) to insert language that permits the FISA court to direct the order to 'other persons' if the court finds that Section 1805(c)(2)(B) of title 50, permits the FISA court to order third parties, like common carriers, custodians, landlords and others, who are specified in the order, (specified persons) to provide assistance and information to law enforcement authorities in the installation of a wiretap or the collection of information related to a foreign intelligence investigation. Section 152 amends 1805(c)(2)(B) to insert language that permits the FISA court to direct the order to 'other persons' if the court finds that the `actions of the target of the application may have the effect of thwarting the identification of a specified person,' who would be required to assist in the installation of any court-authorized intercept. This amendment is intended to expand the existing authority to allow for circumstances where the court finds that the actions of a target may thwart the identification of a specified person in the order. This is usually accomplished by the target moving his location. The move necessitates the use of third parties other than those specified in the original order to assist in installation of the listening device.

"This amendment allows the FISA court to compel any such new necessary parties to assist in the installation and to furnish all information, facilities, or technical assistance necessary without specifically naming such persons. Nevertheless, the target of the electronic surveillance must still be identified or described in the order as under existing law.

"For example, international terrorists and foreign intelligence officers are trained to thwart surveillance by changing hotels, cell phones, Internet accounts, etc. just prior to important meetings or communications. Under present law, each time this happens the government must return to the FISA court for a new order just to change the name of the third party needed to assist in the new installation. The amendment permits the court to issue a generic order that can be presented to the new carrier, landlord or custodian directing their assistance to assure that the surveillance may be undertaken as soon as technically feasible," H.Rept. 107-256, at 59-60 (2001). This section is subject to the sunset provisions of section 224.

Section 207. Duration of FISA Surveillance of Non-United States Persons Who are Agents of a Foreign Power.

Prior to the USA PATRIOT Act, unless directed at a foreign power, FISA surveillance orders and extensions expired after ninety days, and FISA physical search orders and extensions were effective for no more forty-five days, 50 U.S.C. 1805(e), 1824(d)(2000 ed.). Section 207 extends the tenure of physical search orders to ninety days. Surveillance and physical search orders may now remain in effect for up to 120 days with extensions for up to a year, 50 U.S.C. 1805(e), 1824(d). This represents a compromise over the Justice Department's original proposal which would have set the required expiration date for orders at one year instead of 120 days. This section is subject to the sunset provisions of section 224.

Section 208. Designation of Judges.

FISA is in essence a series of procedures available to secure court orders in certain foreign intelligence cases. It operates through a special court which before passage of section 208 consisted of seven judges, scattered throughout the country, two of whom are now from the Washington, D.C. area. Section 208 authorizes the appointment of four additional judges and requires that three members of the court reside within twenty miles of the District of Columbia, 50 U.S.C. 1803(a). This section is not subject to the sunset provisions of section 224.

Section 209. Seizure of Voice-Mail Messages Pursuant to Warrants.

Section 209 treats voice mail like e-mail. Thus, Federal officers may gain access with a warrant or court order. They need no longer resort to the more demanding regime of Title III that applies in the case of live telephone conversations, *United States v. Smith*, 155 F.3d 1050, 1055-56 (9th Cir. 1998). This section is subject to the sunset provisions of section 224.

Section 210. Scope of Subpoenas for Records of Electronic Communications.

"Terrorists and other criminals often use aliases in registering for Internet and telephone services. This creates a problem for law enforcement attempting to identify the suspects of terrorist acts or criminal acts that often support the terrorists. While the government currently can subpoena electronic communications or a remote computing services provider for the name, address and length of service of a suspect, this information does not help when the suspected terrorist or criminal lies about his or her identity. Permitting investigators to obtain credit card and other payment information by a subpoena, along with subscriber information (already permitted to be obtained under current law), will help law enforcement track a suspect and establish his or her true identity.

"This section amend[s] 18 U.S.C. 2703(c) to authorize a subpoena for transactional records to include information regarding the form of payment in order to assist law enforcement in determining the user's identity," H.Rept. 107-236, at 56-7 (2001). This section is not subject to the sunset provisions of section 224.

Section 211. Clarification of Scope.

Telephone and electronic communications providers may be required to provide law enforcement officials with customer identifying information without notifying their customers, 18 U.S.C. 2705(b). Cable companies are prohibited from disclosing customer identifying information without customer approval, 47 U.S.C. 551 *et. seq*. When cable companies began to offer communications services, uncertainty arose over whether law enforcement access to their customers records was to be governed by the standards applicable to the communications industry or by the earlier cable standards, *see In re Application of U.S.A. for an Order Pursuant to 18 U.S.C. 2703(d)*, 158 F.Supp.2d 644 (D.Md. 2001)(holding the cable provisions implicitly repealed and summarizing existing ambivalent case law).

Section 211 resolves the question by amending the Communications Act, 47 U.S.C. 551, to make it clear that when a cable company offers communications services it is subject to the provisions of Title III, and chapters 121 and 206 of title 18 of the United States Code (relating to stored wire and electronic communications and transactional records access and to pen registers and trap and trace devices, respectively). Cable customer video subscription records, however, remain in the shelter of the Communications Act protection. Section 211 is not subject to the sunset provisions of section 224.

Section 212. Emergency Disclosure of Electronic Communications to Protect Life and Limb.

As the House Committee on the Judiciary observed with respect to a substantively identical provision: "This section amends 18 U.S.C. 2702 to authorize electronic communications service providers to disclose the communications (or records relating to such communications) of their customers or subscribers if the provider reasonably believes that an emergency involving immediate danger of death or serious physical injury to any person requires disclosure of the information without delay.

"This section would also amend the law to allow communications providers to disclose non-content information (such as the subscriber's login records). Under current law, the communications provider is expressly permitted to disclose content information but not expressly permitted to provide non-content information. This change would cure this problem and would permit the disclosure of the less-protected information, parallel to the disclosure of the more protected information." H.Rept. 107-236, at 58 (2001). This section is subject to the sunset provisions of section 224.

Section 213. Authority for Delaying Notice of the Execution of a Warrant.

Standing alone, Rule 41 of the Federal Rules of Criminal Procedure seems to preclude delayed notification of the execution of "sneak and peek" warrants. A sneak and peek warrant is one that authorizes officers to secretly enter (either physically or electronically), conduct a search, observe, take measurements, conduct examinations, smell, take pictures, copy documents, download or transmit computer files, and the like; and depart without taking any tangible evidence or leaving notice of their presence. The Rule on its face requires that after the execution of a federal search warrant officers leave a copy of the warrant and an inventory of what they have seized and advise the issuing court what they have done, F.R.Crim.P. 41(d).

The lower federal courts are divided over the extent to which the Rule reflects Fourth Amendment requirements. The Ninth Circuit sees the Fourth Amendment in Rule 41, *United States v. Freitas*, 800 F.2d 1451, 1453 (9th Cir. 1986). The Fourth Circuit finds no Fourth Amendment offense in search warrants secretly executed and seizures of intangible evidence that remain unannounced until weeks thereafter,

United States v. Simons, 206 F.3d 392 (4th Cir. 2000). The Second Circuit, whose views the Congress found persuasive, 147 *Cong.Rec.* H7197 (daily ed. Oct. 23, 2001), thinks the validity of sneak and peek warrants and of delayed notice are better judged by Rule 41 standards, *United States v. Pangburn*, 983 F.2d 449 (2d Cir. 1993).

Section 213 rests on the belief that the Fourth Amendment does not condemn either sneak and peek warrants or delayed notice. For searches conducted under a warrant issued pursuant to Rule 41 or under a warrant or court order issued pursuant to any other rule of law, it adopts the delayed notification standards of 18 U.S.C. 2705 (relating to delayed notification of the execution of a court order authorizing government access to electronic communications held in third party storage for longer than 180 days). An issuing court may order notice delayed for a reasonable period of time and with good cause extensions, if it finds reasonable cause to believe that contemporaneous notification may have any of the adverse consequences described in section 2705. Section 2705 mentions "(A) endangering the life or physical safety of an individual; (B) flight from prosecution; (C) destruction of or tampering with evidence; (D) intimidation of potential witnesses; or (E) otherwise seriously jeopardize an investigation or unduly delay a trial" as the kinds of adverse consequences that justify delay. Unless the court concludes seizure is reasonably necessary, the section only permits delayed notification if the warrant prohibits the seizure of any stored wire or electronic information (unless otherwise authorized), of any tangible property, or of any wire or oral communications. Section 213 is not subject to the sunset provisions of section 224.

Section 214. Pen Register and Trap and Trace Authority Under FISA.

Trap and trace devices and pen registers are devices which secretly identify the source and destination of calls made to and from a particular telephone. Intelligence officers may use them pursuant to a court order authorized in the Foreign Intelligence Surveillance Act. Section 214 grants the request of the Department of Justice for elimination of the requirements which limited FISA pen register and trap and trace device orders to facilities used by foreign agents or those engaged in international terrorist or clandestine intelligence activities, 50 U.S.C. 1842(c)(3)(2000 ed.). Applicants must still certify that the devices are likely to reveal information relevant to a foreign intelligence investigation.

Section 214 also adjusts the language of the FISA pen register-trap and trace authority to permit its use to capture source and destination information for electronic communications (*e.g.*, e-mail) as well as telephone communications, 50 U.S.C. 1842(d). Finally, the section makes it clear that requests for a FISA pen register-trap and trace order, like requests for other FISA orders, directed against Americans and permanent resident aliens (U.S. persons) may not be based solely on activities protected by the First Amendment, 50 U.S.C. 1842, 1843. Section 214 is subject to the sunset provisions of section 224.

Section 215. Access to Records and Other Items Under the Foreign Intelligence Surveillance Act.

FISA previously allowed senior officials of the Federal Bureau of Investigation to apply for a court order, in connection with a foreign intelligence investigation, for access to the records of common carriers, public accommodation providers, physical storage facility operators, and vehicle rental agencies, 50 U.S.C. 1861-1863 (2000 ed.).

Section 215 rewrites those provisions. Assistant Special Agents in Charge of the FBI field offices may now also apply. The court orders extend to any tangible object held by anyone. Items sought need not relate to an identified foreign agent or foreign power as was once the case, but they may only be sought as part of an investigation to protect the United States from international terrorism or clandestine intelligence activities. Nor may they be sought in conjunction with the investigation of an American or permanent resident alien predicated solely on the basis of activities protected by the First Amendment. There is a good faith defense for anyone who produces items in response to a court order under the section and production does not constitute a waiver of applicable privilege. Section 215 is subject to the sunset provisions of section 224.

Section 216. Modification of Authorities Relating to Use of Pen Registers and Trap and Trace Devices.

With one critical exception, Section 216 tracks language in a similar section of H.R. 2975. The House Committee on Judiciary's description of that section is instructive: "Under 18 U.S.C. 3121(b), law enforcement may obtain authorization from a court, upon certification that the information to be obtained is relevant to a pending criminal investigation, to install and use a 'pen register' device that identifies the telephone numbers dialed or pulsed from (outgoing calls) or a 'trap and trace' device that identifies the telephone numbers to a particular telephone (incoming calls). These court authorizations do not permit capturing or recording of the content of any such communication under the terms of the court order.

"Currently, the government must apply for a new pen/trap order in every jurisdiction where the target telephone is located. This can cause serious delays that could be devastating to an investigation, particularly where additional criminal or terrorist acts are planned.

"Section [216] does not change the requirement under 18 U.S.C. 3121 that law enforcement seek a court order to install and use pen registers/trap and trace devices. It does not change the law requiring that the attorney for the government certify to the court that the information sought is relevant to an ongoing criminal investigation.

"This section does change the current law requiring the government to obtain the order in the jurisdiction where the telephone (or its equivalent) is located. This section authorizes the court with jurisdiction over the offense of the investigation to issue the order, thus streamlining an investigation and eliminating the need to intrude upon the resources of courts and prosecutors with no connection to the investigation.

"Under the bill, 18 U.S.C. 3123(a) would authorize courts to issue a single pen register/trap and trace order that could be executed in multiple jurisdictions anywhere in the United States. The bill divides the existing 18 U.S.C. 3123(a) into two paragraphs. The new subsection (a)(1) applies to Federal investigations and provides that the order may be issued to any provider of communication services within the United States whose assistance is appropriate to the effectuation of the order. Subsection (a)(2) applies to State law enforcement and does not change the current authority granted to State officials.

"This section updates the language of the statute to clarify that the pen/register authority applies to modern communication technologies. Current statutory references to the target 'line,' for example, are revised to encompass a 'line or other facility.' Such a facility includes: a cellular telephone number; a specific cellular telephone identified by its electronic serial number (ESN); an Internet user account or e-mail address; or an Internet Protocol (IP) address, port number, or similar computer network address or range of addresses. In addition, because the statute takes into account a wide variety of such facilities, section 3123(b)(1)(C) allows applicants for pen register or trap and trace orders to submit a description of the communications to be traced using any of these or other identifiers.

"Moreover, the section clarifies that orders for the installation of pen register and trap and trace devices may obtain any non-content information – 'dialing, routing, addressing, and signaling information' – utilized in the processing or transmitting of wire and electronic communications.[5] Just as today, such an order could not be used to intercept the contents of communications protected by the wiretap statute. The amendments reinforce the statutorily prescribed line between a communication's contents and non-content information, a line identical to the constitutional distinction drawn by the U.S. Supreme Court in *Smith v. Maryland*, 442 U.S. 735, 741 43 (1979).

"Thus, for example, an order under the statute could not authorize the collection of email subject lines, which are clearly content. Further, an order could not be used to collect information other than 'dialing, routing, addressing, and signaling' information, such as the portion of a URL (Uniform Resource Locator) specifying Web search terms or the name of a requested file or article.

"This concept, that the information properly obtained by using a pen register or trap and trace device is non-content information, applies across the board to all communications media, and to actual connections as well as attempted connections (such as busy signals and similar signals in the telephone context and packets that merely request a telnet connection in the Internet context).

"Further, because the pen register or trap and trace 'device' is often incapable of being physically 'attached' to the target facility due to the nature of modern communication technology, section 101 makes two other related changes. First, in

---

[5] "Thus, for example, non-content information contained in the 'options field' of a network packet header constitutes 'signaling' information and is properly obtained by an authorized pen register or trap and trace device."

recognition of the fact that such functions are commonly performed today by software instead of physical mechanisms, the section allows the pen register or trap and trace device to be 'attached or applied' to the target facility. Likewise, the definitions of 'pen register' and 'trap and trace device' in section 3127 are revised to include an intangible 'process' (such as a software routine) which collects the same information as a physical device.

"Section [216](c) amends the definition section to include a new nexus standard under 3127(2)(A) to provide that the issuing court must have jurisdiction over the crime being investigated rather than the communication line upon which the device is to be installed. This section is also amended to account for the new technologies relating to the different modes of communication.

"Section [216](d) amends section 3124(d) to ensure that communication providers continue to be covered under that section. Technology providers are concerned that the single order provisions of section 101 of the bill eliminates the protection of 3124(d) of title 18 that provides that 'no cause of action shall lie in any court against any provider of a wire or electronic communication service, its officers, employees, agents, or other specified persons for providing information, facilities, or assistance in accordance with the terms of a court order.' Once there is a nation-wide order it will not specify the provider and thus, the providers believe they could become liable upon compliance with the order. The intent of the current statutory language is to protect providers who comply with court orders, which direct them to assist law enforcement in obtaining the non-content information. The bill removes the phrase 'the terms of' so that the phrase reads 'in accordance with a court order.' This will keep the requirement of a court order but protect the providers even when that order does not specify the provider.

"Current practice includes compliance with pen registers and trap and trace orders by the service provider using its systems and technologies to provide the government all non-content information ordered by the order without the installation of an additional device by the government to capture that order. It is intended that these alternative compliance procedures should continue when the provider is willing and technologically able to comply with the order by these means in an efficient, complete and timely manner.

"Additionally, this section clarifies that upon request, those being served with the generic pen/trap order created under this section shall receive written or electronic certification from the serving officer or official stating that the assistance provided is related to the order," H.Rept. 107-236, at 52-4 (2001).

The critical difference in section 216 is its reporting feature. Federal agents executing a pen register or trap and trace order involving an electronic communications service to the public must report the details of the device's installation and use to the issuing court within 30 days of termination of the order. This section is not subject to the sunset provisions of section 224.

Section 217. Interception of Computer Trespasser Communications.

"Cyberattacks may be the work of terrorists or criminals. These attacks come in many forms that cost companies and citizens millions of dollars and endanger public safety. For instance, the denial-of-service attacks, where the objective of the attack is to disable the computer system, can shut down businesses or emergency responders or national security centers. This type of attack causes the target site's servers to run out of memory and become incapable of responding to the queries of legitimate customers or users. The victims of these computer trespasser's should be able to authorize law enforcement to intercept the trespasser's communications. Section [217] amends current law to clarify that law enforcement may intercept such communications when authorized by the victims, under limited circumstances.

"Section [217](1) of the bill adds to the definitions under 18 U.S.C. 2510 the term: (1) ʻprotected computer' and provides that the term has the same meaning set forth in 1030 of title 18; and (2) the term ʻcomputer trespasser' means a person who is accessing a protected computer without authorization and thus has no reasonable expectation of privacy in any communication transmitted to, through, or from the protected computer.

"Section [217](2) of the bill amends current law to allow victims of computer intrusions to authorize law enforcement to intercept the communications of a computer trespasser [that have been transmitted to, from or through the protected computer], under limited circumstances. The circumstances are: (1) the owner or operator of the protected computer must authorize the interception of the trespasser's communications; (2) the person who intercepts the communication must be lawfully engaged in an investigation; (3) the person acting under color of law has reasonable grounds to believe that the contents of the computer trespasser's communication to be intercepted will be relevant to the investigation; and (4) the investigator may only intercept communications of the computer trespasser," H.Rept. 107-236, at 55-6 (2001). This section is subject to the sunset provisions of section 224.

Section 218. Foreign Intelligence Information.

The USA PATRIOT Act contemplates a closer working relationship between criminal and intelligence investigators than has previously been the case. As originally enacted the application for a FISA surveillance order required certification of the fact that "*the* purpose for the surveillance is to obtain foreign intelligence information," 50 U.S.C. 1804(a)(7)(B)(2000 ed.)(emphasis added). From the beginning, defendants have questioned whether authorities had used a FISA surveillance order against them in order to avoid the predicate crime threshold for a Title III order. Out of these challenges arose the notion that perhaps "the purpose" might not always mean the sole purpose.[6]

---

[6] In *United States v. Truong Dinh Hung*, 629 F.2d 908, 915 (4th Cir. 1980), decided after FISA became effective but on the basis of pre-existing law, the court declared, "as the district court ruled, the executive should be excused from securing a warrant only when the surveillance is conducted ʻprimarily' for foreign intelligence reasons. We think that the district court adopted the proper test, because once surveillance becomes primarily a criminal

The Justice Department sought FISA surveillance and physical search authority on the basis of "a" foreign intelligence purpose. Section 218 instead demands certification that foreign intelligence gathering is a "significant purpose" for the FISA surveillance or physical search order application, 50 U.S.C. 1804(a)(7)(B), 1823(a)(7)(B). This a more exacting standard than the "a purpose" threshold proposed by the Justice Department, but a clear departure from the original "the purpose" entry point. FISA once described a singular foreign intelligence focus prerequisite for any FISA surveillance application, a focus that implicitly discouraged law enforcement participation. Section 218 encourages coordination between intelligence and law enforcement officials. Section 504, discussed below, confirms that such coordination is no impediment to a "significant purpose" certification, 50 U.S.C. 1806(k), 1825(k). Section 218 is subject to the sunset provisions of section 224.

Section 219. Single-Jurisdiction Search Warrants for Terrorism.

"Rule 41(a) of the Federal Rules of Criminal Procedure currently requires that a search warrant be obtained within the judicial district where the property to be searched is located. The only exception is where property or a person now in the

---

investigation, the courts are entirely competent to make the usual probable cause determination, and because, importantly, individual privacy interests come to the fore and government foreign policy concerns recede when the government is primarily attempted to form the basis for a criminal prosecution." Subsequent case law, however, is not as clear as it might be: *e.g., United States v. Duggan*, 743 F.2d 59, 77 (2d Cir. 1984)("FISA permits federal officials to obtain orders authorizing electronic surveillance for the purpose of obtaining foreign intelligence information. The requirement that foreign intelligence information be the primary objective of the surveillance is plain not only from the language of Sec. 1802(b) but also from the requirements in Sec. 1804 as to what the application must contain. The application must contain a certification by a designated official of the executive branch that the purpose of the surveillance is to acquire foreign intelligence information, and the certification must set forth the basis for the certifying officials's belief that the information sought is the type of foreign intelligence information described"); *United States v. Pelton*, 835 F.2d 1067, 1075-76 (4th Cir. 1987)("We also reject Pelton's claim that the 1985 FISA surveillance was conducted primarily for the purpose of his criminal prosecution, and not primarily for the purpose of obtaining foreign intelligence information. . . . We agree with the district court that the primary purpose of the surveillance, both initially and throughout was to gather foreign intelligence information. It is clear that otherwise valid FISA surveillance is not tainted simply because the government can anticipate that the fruits of the surveillance may later be used . . . as evidence in a criminal trial"); *United States v. Sarkissian*, 841 F.2d 959, 907-8 (9th Cir. 1988)("Defendants rely on the primary purpose test articulated in *United States v. Truong Dinh Hung*. . . . One other court has applied the primary purpose test. Another court has rejected it . . . distinguishing *Truong*. A third court has declined to decide the issue. We also decline to decide the issue"); *United States v. Johnson*, 952 F.2d 565, 572 (1st Cir. 1991)("Appellants attack the government's surveillance on the ground that it was undertaken not for foreign intelligence purposes, but to gather evidence for a criminal prosecution. FISA applications must contain, among other things, a certification that the purpose of the requested surveillance is the gathering of foreign intelligence information. . . .Although the evidence obtained under FISA subsequently may be used in criminal prosecutions, the investigation of criminal activity cannot be the primary purpose of the surveillance").

district might leave before the warrant is executed. This restriction often causes unnecessary delays and burdens on law enforcement officers investigating terrorist activities that have occurred across multiple judicial districts. These delays can have serious adverse consequences on an ongoing terrorism investigation," H.Rept. 107-236, at 72 (2001).

Section 219 allows a magistrate in the district in which a domestic or international terrorism investigation is being conducted to issue a warrant to be executed either "within or outside the district," F.R.Crim.P. 41(a)(3). Although most useful in criminal investigations spanning a number of states within the United States, nothing in the section expressly precludes its application overseas when the law of the place permits such execution.

The Fourth Amendment does not apply to the overseas searches of the property of foreign nationals, *United States v. Verdugo-Urquidez*, 494 U.S. 259 (1990), but it does reach the search of American property overseas by American authorities, *United States v. Barona*, 56 F.3d 1087, 1092 (9th Cir. 1995). Yet neither Rule 41 nor any other provision of prior federal law apparently contemplated extraterritorial execution of federal search warrants, *cf.*, F.R.Crim.P.41, *Advisory Committee Notes: 1990 Amendment* (discussing a proposal for exterritorial execution that the Supreme Court rejected).[7] Section 219 is not subject to the sunset provisions of section 224.

Section 220. Nationwide Service of Search Warrants for Electronic Evidence.

"Title 18 U.S.C. 2703(a) requires a search warrant to compel service providers to disclose unopened e-mails. This section does not affect the requirement for a search warrant, but rather attempts to address the investigative delays caused by the cross-jurisdictional nature of the Internet. Currently, Federal Rules of Criminal Procedure 41 requires that the 'warrant' be obtained 'within the district' where the property is located. An investigator, for example, located in Boston who is investigating a suspected terrorist in that city, might have to seek a suspect's electronic e-mail from an Internet service provider (ISP) account located in California. The investigator would then need to coordinate with agents, prosecutors and judges in the district in California where the ISP is located to obtain a warrant to search. These time delays could be devastating to an investigation, especially where additional criminal or terrorist acts are planned.

"Section [220] amends 2703 to authorize the court with jurisdiction over the investigation to issue the warrant directly, without requiring the intervention of its

---

[7] The Code does still carry remnants of the consular courts which speak of the overseas execution of arrest warrants in places where the United States has "extraterritorial jurisdiction," 18 U.S.C. 3042. The history of the provision makes it clear that the phrase "extraterritorial jurisdiction" was intended to coincide with those places in which we had consular courts, *see*, S.ReptNo. 73-217, at. 3 (1934), *reprinted*, 78 *Cong.Rec.* 4982-983 (1934)("The countries to which the proposed bill, if enacted into law, would relate are the following, in which the United States exercises extraterritorial jurisdiction: China, Egypt, Ethiopia, Muscat, and Morocco"); 22 U.S.C. 141 (1926 ed.)(conferring judicial powers on consular courts there identified as those located in China, Egypt, Ethiopia, Muscat, Morocco, Siam and Turkey).

counterpart in the district where the ISP is located," H.Rept. 107-236, at 57 (2001). Section 220 is subject to the sunset provisions of section 224.

Section 221. Trade Sanctions.

The Trade Sanctions Reform and Export Enhancement Act of 2000, Title IX of Public Law 106-387, 114 Stat. 1549A-67, restricts the President's authority to impose unilateral agricultural and medical sanctions, subject to certain exceptions. One of the exceptions permits an export ban on products that might be "used to facilitate the development or production of a chemical or biological weapon or weapon of mass destruction,"§904(2)(C). Section 221 amends paragraph 904(2)(C) to enlarge the ban to reach products that might facilitate the *design*, development or production of such weapons. The section amends subsection 906(a) of the trade sanctions act to allow for the sale of agricultural and medical products to entities in Syria and North Korea and to permit such sales under license to areas of Afghanistan controlled by the Taliban.

The section further declares that the trade sanctions act should not be construed to curtail criminal or civil penalties available with respect to the export of agricultural products, medicine, or medical devices in violation of restrictions on dealings with:

• a foreign individual or entity designated pursuant to Executive Order 12947, 50 U.S.C. 1701 note (Prohibiting Transactions With Terrorists);
• a foreign terrorist organization, 18 U.S.C. 2339B;
• a foreign individual or entity designated pursuant to Executive Order 13224, 66 *Fed.Reg.* 49077 (Sept. 25, 2001)(Blocking Property . . . [of] Persons Who . . . Support Terrorism);
• a narcotics trafficker designated pursuant to Executive Order 12979, 50 U.S.C. 1701 note (Blocking Assets . . . With Significant Narcotics Traffickers) or to the Foreign Narcotics Kingpin Designation Act, Public Law 106-120; or
• any foreign individual or entity subject to restriction for involvement in weapons of mass destruction or missile proliferation.

This section is not subject to the sunset provisions of section 224.

Section 222. Assistance to Law Enforcement Agencies.

FISA, Title III, and the related provisions of law now compel communications service providers to assist in the execution of court orders issued under those authorities, *e.g.,* 50 U.S.C. 1805(c)(2)(B), 18 U.S.C. 2518(4). The House Committee on the Judiciary observed with regard to an earlier version of this section that, "this Act is not intended to affect obligations under the Communications Assistance for Law Enforcement Act, 47 U.S.C. 1001 *et seq.,* nor does the Act impose any additional technical obligation or requirement on a provider of wire or electronic communication service or other person to furnish facilities or technical assistance," H.Rept. 107-236, at 62-3 (2001). In its final form, the section guarantees reasonable reimbursement for the costs of service providers, landlords, custodians and others who supply facilities and technical assistance pursuant to section 216 (relating to law enforcement pen registers and trap and trace orders). This section is not subject to the sunset provisions of section 224.

Section 223. Civil Liability of Certain Unauthorized Disclosures.

Section 223 establishes a claim against the United States for not less than $10,000 and costs for violations of Title III, chapter 121, or the Foreign Intelligence Surveillance Act (FISA), and emphasizes the prospect of administrative discipline for offending federal officials. This section is subject to the sunset provisions of section 224.

Section 224. Sunset.

Several of the amendments which grant federal law enforcement or intelligence officers expanded interception powers expire with respect to any foreign intelligence investigation initiated after January 1, 2006 and to any criminal investigation of misconduct occurring only after that date. The provisions which expire are:

- section 201 (authority to intercept wire, oral, and electronic communications relating to terrorism);
- section 202 (authority to intercept wire, oral, and electronic communications relating to computer fraud and abuse offenses);
 subsection 203(b) (authority to share electronic, wire, and oral interception information);
- subsection 203(d) (general authority to share foreign intelligence information);
- section 204 (clarification of intelligence exceptions from limitations on interception and disclosure of wire, oral, and electronic communications);
- section 206 (roving surveillance authority under the Foreign Intelligence Surveillance Act of 1978);
- section 207 (duration of FISA surveillance of non-United States persons who are agents of a foreign power),
- section 209 (seizure of voice-mail messages pursuant to warrants);
- section 212 (emergency disclosure of electronic surveillance);
- section 214 (pen register and trap and trace authority under FISA);
- section 215 (access to records and other items under the Foreign Intelligence Surveillance Act);
- section 217 (interception of computer trespasser communications);
- section 218 (foreign intelligence information);
- section 220 (nationwide service of search warrants for electronic evidence);
- section 223 (civil liability for certain unauthorized disclosures); and
- section 225 (immunity for compliance with FISA wiretap).

The permanent sections and subsections of title II, which do not expire, are:

- subsection 203(a) (sharing grand jury information);
- subsection 203(c) (Attorney General guidelines for sharing grand jury information);
- section 205 (employment of FBI translators);
- section 208 (number and residence of FISA court judges);
- section 210 (nation wide subpoenas for electronic communications records),
- section 211 (clarification of scope of cable provider obligations);
- section 213 (delayed notification of sneak and peek warrant execution);

❗ section 216 (modification of authorities relating to pen registers and trap and trace devices);

❗ section 219 (single-jurisdiction search warrants for terrorism);

❗ section 221 (trade sanctions); and

❗ section 222 (assistance to law enforcement agencies).

Section 225. Immunity for Compliance With FISA Wiretap.

The Foreign Intelligence Surveillance Act orders may include instructions requiring communications service providers and others to assist officers in the execution of the order, 50 U.S.C. 1805(c)(2)(B), 1824(c)(2)(B), 1842(c)(2)(B). Section 225 immunizes those who do from civil liability, 50 U.S.C. 1805(h). This section is subject to the sunset provisions of section 224.

Title III – International Money Laundering Abatement and Anti-Terrorist Financing Act of 2001[8]

Section 301. Short Title.

The popular name for Title III of the USA PATRIOT Act is the International Money Laundering Abatement and Financial Anti-Terrorism Act of 2001.

Section 302. Findings and Purposes.

Section 302 describes the findings and purposes for the enactment of the International Money Laundering Abatement and Financial Anti-Terrorism Act.

Section 303. 4-Year Congressional Review; Expedited Consideration.

The International Money Laundering Abatement and Financial Anti-Terrorism Act of this title will sunset after four years upon passage of joint resolution of repealed. Any joint resolution of repeal is to be afforded "fact track" consideration.

Subtitle A–International Counter Money Laundering and Related Measures

Section 311. Special Measures for Jurisdictions, Financial Institutions, or International Transactions of Primary Money Laundering Concern.

Section 311 authorizes the Secretary of the Treasury (the Secretary) to impose certain regulatory restrictions, known as "special measures," upon finding that a jurisdiction outside the U.S., a financial institution outside the U.S., a class of transactions involving a jurisdiction outside the U.S., or a type of account, is "of

---

[8] M.Maureen Murphy, a legislative attorney in the American Law Division prepared the section by section analysis of Title III.

primary money laundering concern." To make this finding, the Secretary must consult with the Secretary of State and the Attorney General and consider certain factors relating to the foreign jurisdiction or the particular institution targeted. Among the factors relating to a jurisdiction are: involvement with organized crime or terrorists, bank secrecy laws and regulations, the existence a mutual legal assistance treaty with the U.S., and level of official corruption. The special measures generally involve detailed record keeping and reporting requirements relating to underlying transactions and beneficial ownership of accounts. Special measures could involve prohibiting the maintenance of payable-through or correspondent accounts for such institutions or jurisdictions, provided that there has been consultation with the Secretary of State, the Attorney General, and the Chairman of the Federal Reserve Board, as well as with other appropriate federal banking agencies and consideration has been given to whether other nations have taken similar action, whether there would be a significant competitive disadvantage on U.S. financial institutions, and effect upon the international payment system. "Account" is defined for banks, with authority delegated to the Secretary to define the term for other financial services businesses upon consultation with the appropriate federal regulators. The Secretary is required to issue a regulation defining "beneficial ownership" for purposes of this legislation.

Section 312. Special Due Diligence for Correspondent Accounts and Private Banking Accounts.

Section 312 requires every financial institution with a private banking or correspondent account for a foreign person or bank to establish policies and controls designed to detect and report money laundering through the accounts. If a correspondent account is maintained for a foreign bank that operates under an offshore license–*i.e.*, does not and may not do banking business in the chartering country–or that is licensed by a jurisdiction designated for special measures or listed as non-cooperative by an international organization in which the U.S. participates and concurs, enhanced due diligence policies are required. For correspondent accounts for foreign banks, U.S. banks, at the minimum, must secure ownership information on the foreign bank, maintain enhanced scrutiny of the account, and ascertain due diligence information on the foreign banks for which the target bank provides correspondent banking services. For foreign private banking clients, *i.e.*, those with aggregated deposits of $1,000,000, information must be secured on the identity of the owners of the accounts, including beneficial owners, and the source of the funds; enhanced scrutiny is required for accounts held for senior foreign political figures. This section becomes effective 9 months after enactment; regulations must be issued within 6 months of enactment.

Section 313. Prohibition on United States Correspondent Accounts with Foreign Shell Banks.

Section 313 prohibits U.S. banks, thrifts, private banks, foreign bank agencies and branches operating in the U.S., and brokers and dealers licensed under the Securities Exchanges Act of 1934, 15 U.S.C. 78a *et seq.*, from maintaining correspondent accounts for foreign shell banks–banks that have no physical presence in any country. It requires that the covered institutions take reasonable steps to preclude their providing services to such shell banks through other banks and requires the Secretary to issue implementing regulations.

Section 314. Cooperative Efforts to Deter Money Laundering.

Section 314 requires the Secretary to issue regulations within 120 days of enactment to encourage further cooperation among financial institutions and regulatory and law enforcement authorities to promote sharing information on individuals, entities, and organizations engaged in or suspected of engaging in terrorist acts or money laundering. In these regulations, the Secretary may require each financial institution to designate persons to receive information and to monitor accounts and to establish procedures to protect the shared information.   No information received by a financial institution under this provision may be used for any purpose other than identifying and reporting activities involving terrorism or money laundering. If a financial institution uses this information for those purposes, it may not be held liable for unauthorized disclosure or failure to provide a notice under any law or regulation, state or federal, or any contract or agreement. The Secretary is required to provide a semiannual report analyzing suspicious activity reports.

Section 315.   Inclusion of Foreign Corruption Offenses As Money Laundering Crimes.

Section 315 adds to the list of offenses under foreign law, the proceeds of which may form an element of a federal money laundering prosecution: any crime of violence; bribery of a public official; theft, embezzlement, or misappropriation of public funds; certain smuggling or export control violations; and, offenses for which the U.S. would be obliged to extradite alleged offenders. Also added would be certain offenses under the U.S. criminal code relating to customs, importation of firearms, firearms trafficking, computer fraud and abuse, and felony violations of the Foreign Agents Registration Act.

Section 316. Anti-Terrorist Forfeiture Protection.

Prior to enactment of the USA PATRIOT Act, the President had authority to order the vesting of seized foreign assets under the Trading With the Enemy Act §5(b), 50 U.S.C. App. 5(b), which applies when there has been a declaration of war, but not under the International Emergency Economic Powers Act (IEEPA), 50 U.S. C. 1702), which applies when the President has declared the existence of an unusual or extraordinary threat to the U.S. national security, foreign policy, or economy having its source, in whole or substantial part, outside the United States. Section 106 of the new law amends IEEPA to authorize the President, "when the United States is engaged in armed hostilities or has been attacked by a foreign country or foreign nationals," to "confiscate any property, subject to the jurisdiction of the United States, of any foreign person, foreign organization, or foreign country that he determines has planned, authorized, aided, or engaged in such hostilities or attacks against the United States."

Section 316 authorizes judicial review of confiscation of terrorist related assets and sets forth two defenses for those claiming the property that must be proven by a preponderance of the evidence: (1) that the property is not subject to forfeiture under the applicable law, and (2) the innocent owner defense detailed in the criminal forfeiture provision of 18 U.S.C. 983(d). It also authorizes the government to offer otherwise inadmissible evidence provided the court finds that complying with the

Federal Rules of Evidence would jeopardize national security. There is also a clause alluding to the right to raise Constitutional claims and claims under the Administrative Procedure Act and a savings clause preserving other remedies.

Section 317. Long-Arm Jurisdiction Over Foreign Money Launderers.

Section 317 provides jurisdiction over foreign persons, including financial institutions, for substantive money laundering offenses under 18 U.S.C. 1956 and 1957, provided there is a valid service of process and either the offense involved a transaction in the U.S. or the property has been the subject of a forfeiture judgment or a criminal sentence. The district courts are authorized to appoint a receiver to take control of the property.

Section 318. Laundering Money Through a Foreign Bank.

Section 318 amends the substantive money laundering criminal statute, 18 U.S.C. 1956, to cover laundering money through a foreign bank.

Section 319. Forfeiture of Funds in United States Interbank Accounts.

Section 319 amends 18 U.S.C. 981 to permit forfeiture, including forfeiture under the Controlled Substances laws, of accounts in offshore offices of foreign banks by substituting funds in interbank accounts in U.S. financial institutions up to the value of the funds in the targeted account. The section authorizes the Attorney General to suspend or terminate such a forfeiture action on conflict-of-law grounds or upon a finding that to do so would be in the interest of justice and would not harm the national interests of the U.S.

Section 319, effective within 60 days of enactment, amends the Currency and Transaction Reporting Act, 31 U.S.C. 5311, *et seq.*, to require U.S. banks, thrifts, private banks, foreign bank agencies and branches operating in the U.S., and brokers and dealers licensed under the Securities Exchanges Act of 1934, 15 U.S.C. 78a *et seq.*, to provide federal regulators, upon request, information on the institution's compliance with anti-money laundering requirements or on a customer's account, within 120 hours. It also authorizes the Secretary of the Treasury or the Attorney General to subpoena records from a foreign bank that has a correspondent account in the U.S. that relate to that account, including records maintained abroad. It requires U.S. institutions maintaining correspondent accounts for foreign banks to maintain records identifying the owners of such foreign banks and indicating the name and address of a U.S. resident authorized to accept service of legal process for records relating to the correspondent account. U.S. institutions having such correspondent accounts are required to provide federal law enforcement officers with these names and addresses within 7 days of receiving a request and are required to terminate correspondent accounts within 10 business days of receiving a notice from the Secretary or the Attorney General that the foreign bank has failed to comply with a subpoena or to contest its issuance. U.S. financial institutions are not to be held liable for terminating such accounts and are subject to civil penalties of $10,000 per day for failing to do so.

This section also amends the criminal forfeiture provisions of the Controlled Substances Act, 21 U.S.C. 853(p) and 853(e) to permit a court to order return to the jurisdiction of substitute assets, property that may be substituted for unreachable property subject to forfeiture, and to issue a pre-trial order to a defendant to repatriate such substitute assets.

Section 320. Proceeds of Foreign Crimes.

Section 320 authorizes the forfeiture of property derived from or traceable to violations of felonious foreign controlled substances laws, provided the offense is punishable by death or a term of imprisonment of more than one year under the law of the foreign nation and under U.S. law, had it occurred within the jurisdiction of the U.S.

Section 321. Financial Institutions Specified in Subchapter II of Chapter 53 of Title 31, United States Code.

Section 321 adds credit unions and CFTC-regulated or registered futures commission merchants, commodity trading advisors, and commodity pool operators to the specific list of financial institutions subject to the requirements of the Currency and Foreign Transaction Reporting Act. Pre-existing law did not specifically include these entities although it delegated broad authority to the Secretary to apply the requirements to "any other business ... whose cash transactions have a high degree of usefulness in criminal, tax, or regulatory matters."

Section 322. Corporation Represented by a Fugitive.

Section 322 amends 28 U.S.C. 2466 to include corporations having a majority stockholder who is a fugitive, thus, disallowing such corporations to file innocent owner to successfully pursue innocent owner claims in a civil or criminal forfeiture cases.

Section 323. Enforcement of Foreign Judgments.

Section 323 amends 28 U.S.C. 2467 to extend authority for judicial enforcement of foreign confiscation from the previous provisions limiting such enforcement to confiscations related to drug trafficking offenses. Under the newly enacted provision U.S. district courts may enforce foreign confiscations related to any offense under foreign law that, if committed under U.S. law, would have permitted forfeiture.

Section 324. Report and Recommendation.

Section 324 requires the Secretary of the Treasury, within 30 months of enactment, to report on operations respecting the provisions relating to international counter-money laundering measures and any recommendations to Congress as to advisable   legislative   action.

Section 325. Concentration Accounts at Financial Institutions.

Section 325 authorizes the Secretary of the Treasury to prescribe regulations governing maintenance of concentration accounts by financial institutions. If issued, such regulations must prohibit financial institutions from allowing clients to direct transactions through those accounts, prohibit financial institutions from informing customers of the means of identifying such accounts, and require each financial institution to establish written procedures to document all transactions involving a concentration account that amounts belonging to each customer may be identified.

Section 326. Verification of Identification.

Section 326 requires the Secretary of the Treasury, jointly with appropriate regulators of financial institutions, within a year of enactment, to prescribe minimum standards for identifying customers opening accounts at financial institutions. These are to include procedures to verify customer identity and maintain records of information used to verify identity. They are also to require that government lists of terrorists and terrorist organizations be consulted. Under this section, the Secretary is required to submit a report to Congress within six months of enactment, recommending a means of insuring similarly accurate identification of foreign nationals, requiring an identification number similar to a Social Security number or a tax identification number for foreign nationals opening accounts at financial institutions, and setting up a system for financial institutions to review information held by government agencies to verify identities of foreign nationals opening accounts.

Section 327. Consideration of Anti-Money Laundering Record.

Section 327 amends the Bank Holding Company Act and The Federal Deposit Insurance Act, to require that, before approving certain acquisition or merger applications under the Bank Holding Company Act or the Federal Deposit Insurance Act, the Board of Governors of the Federal Reserve System and the Federal Deposit Insurance Corporation must consider the institution's effectiveness in combating money laundering.

Section 328. International Cooperation on Identification of Originators of Wire Transfers.

Section 328 requires the Secretary of the Treasury to encourage foreign governments to require the name of the originator in wire transfer instructions and include it from origination to disbursement. The Secretary is to report annually on progress toward this end to House Financial Services Committee and Senate Banking, Housing, and Urban Affairs Committee.

Section 329. Criminal Penalties.

Section 329 criminalizes the soliciting of a bribe by anyone acting on behalf of an entity of the Federal Government in connection with the administration of the International Money Laundering Abatement and Anti-Terrorist Financing Act of 2001, subject to a fine of up to three time the value of the thing of value constituting the bribe, 15 years imprisonment, or both.

Section 330. International Cooperation in Investigations of Money Laundering, Financial Crimes, and the Finances of Terrorist Groups.

Section 330 states the sense of Congress that international negotiations should be pursued for further cooperative efforts to insure that foreign financial institutions maintain adequate records relating to foreign terrorist organizations and money launderers and make such records available to U.S. law enforcement officials and domestic financial institution supervisors.

Subtitle B–Bank Secrecy Act Amendments and Related Improvements

Section 351. Amendments Relating to Reporting of Suspicious Activities.

Section 351 amends the Currency and Foreign Transactions Reporting Act, 31 U.S.C. 5318(g)(3), to extend the safe harbor provisions for financial institutions and their employees who provide information as to possible law violations to cover all voluntary disclosures of possible law violations made to any federal government agency. Also covered are employees or agents of institutions who require others to make such disclosures. The immunity provided under the legislation covers potential liability under contracts and other legally enforceable agreements. Previously, immunity was provided only for disclosures of violation of law or regulation pursuant to law or regulation; there was no specific immunity for those requiring others to make disclosures; and, immunity extended only to liability under laws or regulations of the United States or constitution, law, or regulation of a state or political subdivision thereof. The section makes it clear that the liability does not extend to prosecutions brought by governmental entities. Disclosure to the subject of the tip-off is prohibited. Information disclosed about potential law violations may be used in employment references to other financial institutions as well as, under the rules of the securities exchanges, in termination notices.

Section 352. Anti-Money Laundering Programs.

Section 352, effective 180 days after enactment, requires each financial institution to develop an anti-money laundering program to include development of internal policies, designation of a compliance officer, ongoing employee training, and an independent audit function to test the programs. It authorizes the Secretary of the Treasury to prescribe minimum standards for such programs and to exempt those financial institutions that are not covered by the regulations promulgated under the Currency and Foreign Transactions Reporting Act. It requires the Secretary to prescribe regulations that consider the extent to which the requirements imposed under this section comport with the size, location, and activities of the financial institutions to which they apply.

Section 353. Penalties for Violations of Geographic Targeting Orders and Certain Recordkeeping Requirements, and Lengthening Effective Period of Geographic Targeting Orders.

Section 353 extends the civil and criminal penalties under the Currency and Foreign Transactions Reporting Act, 31 U.S.C. 5321(a) and 5322, to include violations of geographic targeting orders issued under that Act and willful violations of regulations prescribed under the record keeping requirements of the Bank Secrecy Act, found in Section 21 of the FDIA, 12 U.S.C. 1829(b), or violations of regulations covering uninsured financial institutions issued by Treasury under the authority of 12 U.S.C. 1951 - 1959. Before enactment of USA-PATRIOT, 12 U.S.C. 1829(b) carried no criminal penalties and set civil penalties for violations of regulations issued under 12 U.S.C. 1829(b) at up to $10,000. Section 1955 of Title 12, U.S.C. carried civil penalties of up to $10,000; and, 12 U.S.C. 1956 carried a criminal penalty of up to $1,000 and imprisonment for one year. 31 U.S.C. 5321(a) permits civil penalties of $25,000 or the amount of the instrument (not to exceed $100,000); 31 U.S.C. 5322 permits criminal penalties of up to $250,000 in fines and imprisonment of up to 5 years for a single offense and enhancement for offenses committed in conjunction with other offenses or as a pattern of criminal activity.

The section also extends the prohibitions on structuring transactions to avoid reporting requirements, 31 U.S.C. 5324, to cover structuring to avoid geographic targeting orders and record keeping requirements of the Bank Secrecy Act, found in Section 21 of the FDIA, 12 U.S.C. 1829(b) and 12 U.S.C. 1951- 1959. It extends the permissible length of geographic targeting orders from 60 to 180 days.

Section 354. Anti-Money Laundering Strategy.

Section 354 includes among the areas suggested for inclusion in the annual anti-money laundering strategy data regarding the funding of international terrorism acts.

Section 355. Authorization to Include Suspicions of Illegal Activity in Written Employment References.

Section 355 authorizes depository institutions, "[n]otwithstanding any other provision of law," to disclose the possible involvement of institution-affiliated parties in potentially unlawful activity. Such disclosures may be made to other insured depository institutions requesting employment references, provided the disclosure is not made with malicious intent.

Section 356. Reporting of Suspicious Activities Reports by Securities Brokers and Dealers; Investment Company Study.

Section 356 requires the Secretary of the Treasury, by January 1, 2002, to publish proposed regulations requiring registered brokers and dealers to file suspicious activity reports under 31 U.S.C. 5318(g). It also authorizes the Secretary to prescribe such regulations for futures commission merchants, commodity trading advisors, and commodity pool operators registered under the Commodity Exchange Act. It also requires a report, within one year of enactment, recommending effective regulations under the Currency and Foreign Transactions Reporting Act for investment companies, as defined in the Investment Company Act of 1940, and to evaluate the possibility of requiring trusts and personal holding companies to disclose their beneficial owners when opening accounts at depository institutions.

Section 357. Special Report on Administration of Bank Secrecy Provisions.

Section 357 requires the Secretary of the Treasury to submit a report, within six months of enactment, on the role of the Internal Revenue Service in administering the Bank Secrecy Act's Currency and Foreign Transactions Reporting Act. The report is specifically to address such issues as whether processing of information is to be shifted from the Internal Revenue Service and whether the Internal Revenue Service is to retain authority for auditing money services and gaming businesses' compliance.

Section 358. Bank Secrecy Provisions and Activities of United States Intelligence Agencies to Fight International Terrorism.

Section 358 authorizes the Secretary of the Treasury to refer suspicious activity reports to U.S. intelligence agencies for use in the conduct of intelligence or counterintelligence activities to protect against international terrorism. It authorizes the release of information under the Currency and Foreign Transactions Reporting Act and other provisions of the Bank Secrecy Act, the Right to Financial Privacy Act, and the Fair Credit Reporting Act, to U.S. intelligence agencies by amending 31 U.S.C. 5311, 5318(g)(4)(b), 5319; 12 U.S.C. 1829(b), 1953; 12 U.S.C. 3412(a); 15 U.S.C. 1681x.

Section 359. Reporting of Suspicious Activities by Underground Banking Systems.

Section 359 specifically includes "a licensed sender of money or any other person who engages as a business in the transmission of funds, including any person who engages as a business in an informal money transfer system or any network of people who engage as a business in facilitating the transfer of money domestically or internationally outside of the conventional financial institutions system" as a "financial institution" subject to the requirements of the Currency and Foreign Transactions Reporting Act. It subjects them to any regulations promulgated under the authority of section 21 of the Federal Deposit Insurance Act, 12 U.S.C. 1829b. That section of the law provides authority for the regulations issued under 31 C.F.R. Part 103, requiring reports of currency and foreign transactions, including those requiring suspicious activity reports from money services businesses, 31 C.F.R. § 103.20. Section 359 also mandates a report by the Secretary, within a year of enactment, on whether further legislation is needed with respect to these underground banking systems, including whether the threshold for reporting suspicious activities ($2,000) should be lowered for them.

Section 360. Use of Authority of United States Executive Directors.

Section 360 authorizes the President to direct the U. S. Executive Directors of international financial institutions to use their voice and vote to support countries or entities that have contributed to the U.S. anti-terrorism efforts and ensure that no funds of their institutions are paid to persons who threaten to commit or support terrorism. International financial institutions, as defined in 22 U.S.C. 262r(c)(2), include the International Monetary Fund, the International Bank for Reconstruction, the European Bank for Reconstruction and Development, the International Development Association, the International Finance Corporation, the Multilateral Investment Guarantee Agency, the African Development Bank, the African Development Fund, the Asian Development Bank, the Bank for Economic Development and Cooperation in the Middle East and North Africa, and the InterAmerican Investment Corporation.

Section 361. Financial Crimes Enforcement Network (FinCEN).

Section 361, by enacting 31 U.S.C. 310, transforms FinCEN from a Treasury Department bureau established administratively to a statutory bureau in the Treasury Department. It specifies that it is to be headed by a Director to be appointed by the Secretary. It details its duties and powers, not all of which are summarized here. Subject to applicable legal requirements and guidance by Treasury, FinCEN is to maintain a government-wide data access service to information collected under the anti-money laundering reporting laws, information on currency flows, and other records maintained by other government offices as well as privately and publically available information. It is to analyze and disseminate data : (1) to federal, state, local, and foreign law enforcement officials to identify possible criminal activity; and (2) to regulatory officials to identify possible violations of the anti-money laundering reporting requirements. It is to determine emerging trends and methods in money laundering, and support intelligence activities against international terrorism.

FinCEN is to establish and maintain a financial crimes communications center to furnish law enforcement authorities with intelligence information relating to investigations and undercover operations. It is to furnish informational services to financial institutions, federal regulatory agencies, and law enforcement authorities, in the interest of countering terrorism, organized crime, money laundering, and other financial crimes. It is to assist law enforcement and regulatory authorities in combating the use of informal nonbank networks permitting transfer of funds or the equivalent of funds without records and in insuring compliance with criminal and tax laws. It is to provide computer and data support and data analysis to the Secretary of the Treasury for tracking and controlling foreign assets. It is to administer the anti-money laundering reporting requirements as delegated by the Secretary of the Treasury.

Section 361 further specifies that the Secretary is to proscribe procedures with respect to the government-wide data access service and the financial crimes communications center maintained by FinCEN to provide efficient entry, retrieval, and dissemination of information. This is to include a method for submitting reports by Internet, cataloguing of information, and prompt initial review of suspicious activity reports. Section 361 requires the Secretary to develop, in accordance with the Privacy Act, 5 U.S.C. 552a, and the Right to Financial Privacy Act, 12 U.S.C. 3401, *et seq.*, procedures for determining access, limits on use, and "how information about activities or relationships which involve or are closely associated with the exercise of constitutional rights are screened out."

Appropriations of such sums as are necessary are authorized for fiscal years through 2005.

The Secretary is to study methods for improving compliance with the reporting requirements under 31 U.S.C. 5314, relating to foreign currency transactions, and to submit an annual report to Congress on the subject, beginning six months after enactment.

Section 362. Establishment of Highly Secure Network.

Section 362 requires the Secretary to establish as operational within nine months, a highly secure network in FinCEN to allow financial institutions to file electronically reports required under the Bank Secrecy Act and to provide financial institutions with alerts and other information regarding suspicious activities warranting immediate and enhanced scrutiny.

Section 363. Increase in Civil and Criminal Penalties for Money Laundering.

Section 363 amends 31 U.S.C. 5321(a) and 5322 to permit the Secretary to impose a civil money penalty and a court to impose a criminal penalty equal to 2 times the amount of the transaction, but not more than $1,000,000 for violations of the suspicious activity reporting requirements, under 31 U.S.C. 5318(i) and (j) or any special measures imposed under 31 U.S.C. 5318A. Under pre-existing law, the Secretary had authority to impose a civil money penalty of the amount of the transaction, up to $100,000, or $25,000; and, a criminal fine for a violation of the suspicious activity reporting requirement was set at not more than $250,000.

Section 364. Uniform Protection Authority for Federal Reserve Facilities.

Section 364 authorizes the Federal Reserve Board to issue regulations, subject to the approval of the Attorney General, to authorize personnel to act as law enforcement officers to protect the Board's personnel, property, and operations, including the Federal Reserve banks, and for such personnel to carry firearms and make arrests. Pre-existing law provided no such authority.

Section 365. Reports Relating to Coins and Currency Received in Non-Financial Trade of Business.

Section 365 adds a new section to the anti-money laundering reporting requirements, 31 U.S.C. 5331. It requires anyone engaging in a trade or business, who receives $10,000 in coins or currency (including foreign currency and financial instruments) in a single transaction or in two related transactions to file a report on the transaction to FinCEN as prescribed by the Secretary in regulations. The form for such reports must include the name and address of the person from whom the coins or currency are received, the date and nature of the transaction, and such other information as the Secretary may prescribe. Exemptions are made for reports filed by financial institutions under 31 U.S.C. 5313 and its implementing regulations, and for transactions occurring outside the United States–unless the Secretary so prescribes. The section also includes a provision that prohibits structuring transactions to cause such businesses to evade these reporting requirements or requirements under implementing regulations.[9] "Nonfinancial trade or business" is defined to mean any trade or business other than a financial institution subject to reporting requirements under 31 U.S.C. 5313 and regulations thereunder.

Under pre-existing law, the Secretary had broad authority to apply the reporting requirements of 31 U.S.C. 5313 by regulation. Under 31 U.S.C. 5312 "financial institution" is defined explicitly to include many non-financial businesses including vehicle sales, real estate closings, the United States Postal Service, and casinos. 31 U.S.C. 5312(a)(2)(T), (U), (V), and (X). It also may include any business or agency determined by the Secretary to engage in an activity that is a substitute for any of the activities listed as "financial institutions," and "any other business designated by the Secretary whose cash transactions have a high degree of usefulness in criminal, tax, or regulatory matters." 31 U.S.C. 5312(a)(2)(Z) and (Y). The Secretary has, thus far, not chosen to exercise this power broadly. The new law provides even more comprehensive authority but does not require reports until regulations are issued.

Section 366. Efficient Use of Currency Transaction Report System.

Section 366 requires the Secretary to study expanding the statutory exemption system to the currency transaction reporting requirements , under 31 U.S.C. 5313, authorizing exemptions for transactions with various entities and qualified business customers from the domestic currency and coin reporting requirements. The study is to address methods for improving financial institutions' use of these exemptions to reduce the submission of reports with little or no value for law enforcement purposes. A report on this is required within one year.

Subtitle C–Currency Crimes and Protection

Section 371. Bulk Cash Smuggling into or out of the United States.

Section 371 creates a new criminal offense, knowingly concealing more than $10,000 and transporting it or attempting to transfer it out of or into the United States. Conviction under the statute is subject to imprisonment for up to 5 years and forfeiture of any property involved in the offense. Preexisting law, 31 U.S.C. 5316, requires a report by anyone transporting monetary instruments, defined to include currency, of more than $10,000 into or out of the U.S. In *United States v. Bajakajian*, 524 U.S. 324 (1998), the Supreme Court ruled it unconstitutional to require forfeiture of $357,144, in cash that the defendant possessed legitimately and was attempting to carry with him when leaving the United States. The Court found the penalty disproportional to the gravity of the offense and a violation of the Excessive Fines Clause of the Eighth Amendment to the U. S. Constitution. In reaching that decision, the Court considered the fact that the offense was merely a reporting offense since it was not illegal to transport the currency.

---

[9] There appears to be a typographical error in the text of the legislation. The prohibition on structuring refers to 31 U.S.C. 5333, rather than to 5331.

Section 372. Forfeiture in Currency Reporting Cases.

Section 372 authorizes criminal forfeiture and civil forfeitures for violations of the reporting requirements relating to monetary instruments and makes the criminal forfeiture procedures of section 413 of the Controlled Substances Act and the civil forfeiture procedures of 18 U.S.C. 981(a)(1)(A) (money laundering) applicable to criminal and civil forfeiture, respectively, under 31 U.S.C. 5313 (reports on domestic coins and currency), 5316 (reports on exporting monetary instruments), and 5324 (structuring transactions to evade reporting requirements). Pre-existing law authorized forfeiture of any property involved in the transaction in violation of 31 U.S.C. 5324(b) (international monetary instruments) or property traceable to such property under customs procedures, as held by the court in *United States v. Twenty Thousand Seven Hundred Fifty-Seven Dollars and Eight-Three Cents ($20,757.83) Canadian Currency*, 769 F. 2d 479 (8th Cir. 1985).

Section 373. Illegal Money Transmitting Businesses.

Section. 373 prohibits anyone from knowingly conducting, controlling, managing, supervising, directing, or owning a money transmitting business: (1) without a license in a state that requires such a license and subjects operating without a licence to state misdemeanor or felony penalties; (2) not registered with Treasury under 31 U.S.C. 5330; or (3) involves the transportation or transmission of funds that the defendants knows to have been derived from a criminal offense or are intended to be used to promote or support unlawful activity. The section prescribes a federal penalty of up to five years' imprisonment and criminal fines and authorizes civil forfeiture of property involved in transactions in connection with this offense.

Under the Money Laundering Suppression Act of 1994, 31 U.S.C. 5330(a), the Secretary of the Treasury is required to establish a system to register money transmitting businesses. FinCEN's regulations require registration by December 31, 2001. 31 C.F.R. §103.41.

Section 374. Counterfeiting Domestic Currency and Obligations.

Section 374 extends the definition of counterfeiting obligations of the United States to cover analog, digital, or electronic images, as well as "any plate, stone, or other thing or part thereof, used to counterfeit" such obligations or securities, as provided in pre-existing law, 18 U.S.C. 470(2). This section is also amended to provide similar penalties for offenses committed outside the U.S. as are applicable to those within the U.S. Other provisions increase the penalties under other counterfeiting statutes to 20 years' imprisonment: 18 U.S.C. 471 (obligations or securities of the U.S.); 472 (uttering counterfeit obligations or securities); 473 (dealing in counterfeit obligations or securities); and, 474 (using plates or stones for counterfeiting).

The section amends 18 U.S.C. 474 to cover counterfeiting involving an analog, digital or electronic image of U.S. obligations, unless authorized by Treasury. It amends 18 U.S.C. 476 (taking impressions of tools used for obligations or securities of the U.S.) to increase the penalty from 10 years to 25 years' imprisonment. It amends 18 U.S.C. 477 (possessing or selling impressions of tools used for obligations or securities) to cover an analog, digital, or electronic image. It raises the penalty for connecting parts of different notes, 18 U.S.C. 484, from five years' to ten years' imprisonment, and for offenses under 18 U.S.C. 493 (bonds and obligations of certain lending agencies), from five to ten years' imprisonment.

Section 375. Counterfeiting Foreign Currency and Obligations.

Section 375 increases the penalties for violations of various offenses involving foreign currency and obligations as follows: 18 U.S.C. 478 (foreign obligations or securities, penalty raised from five to 20 years); 18 U.S.C. 479 (uttering counterfeit foreign obligations, penalty raised from three to 20 years); 18 U.S.C. 480 (possessing counter foreign obligations or securities, penalty raised from one to 20 years); 18 U.S.C. 481 (plates or stones for counterfeiting foreign obligations or securities, penalty raised from five to 20 years); 18 U.S.C. 482 (foreign bank notes, penalty raised from two to twenty years); and 18 U.S.C. 483 (foreign bank notes, penalty raised from two to 20 years). The section also criminalizes counterfeiting involving an analog, digital, or electronic image of foreign obligations and securities. It adds 18 U.S.C. 2339B, providing material support to designated foreign terrorist organizations as a predicate for a money laundering prosecution under 18 U.S.C. 1956.

Section 377. Extraterritorial Jurisdiction.

Section 377 enhances the applicability of 18 U.S.C. 1029 (computer fraud) by covering offenses committed outside the U.S. that involve an access device issued by a U.S. entity, such as a credit card, provided the defendant transports, delivers, conveys, transfers to or through, or otherwise stores, secrets, or holds within the jurisdiction of the U.S., any article used to assist in the commission of the offense or the proceeds of such offense or property derived therefrom.

Title IV – Protecting the Border

Subtitle A – Protecting the Northern Border

Section 401. Ensuring Adequate Personnel on the Northern Border.

Annual appropriation legislation ordinarily authorizes the number of work years ("full time equivalents") that an agency may devote to a particular mission. Section 401 authorizes the Attorney General to waive the limitation applicable to Immigration and Naturalization Service (INS) personnel assigned to the Northern Border.

Section 402. Northern Border Personnel.

Section 402 authorizes appropriations in the amounts necessary to triple the number of Border Patrol, Custom Service, and the Immigration and Naturalization Service (INS) personnel in each state along the Northern Border of the United States. It authorizes appropriations of an additional $50 million each for INS and the

Customs Service to improve and supplement their monitoring equipment at the Northern Border.

Section 403. Access by the Department of State and the INS to Certain Identifying Information in the Criminal History Records of Visa Applicants and Applicants for Admission to the United States.

Section 403 authorizes the appropriations necessary to provide the State Department and INS with access to the Federal Bureau of Investigation's automated National Criminal Information Files and to permit the National Institute of Standards and Technology to development the standards necessary to accommodate the transfer of information. All United States consular officers responsible for issuing visas, border inspection officers, and law enforcement and intelligence officers with alien investigation and identification responsibilities will use access to ensure that applicants for entry into the United States have no criminal record here. The FBI will provide access without charge except, at least initially, for fingerprint processing. The Secretary of State will promulgate regulations to ensure the confidentiality and appropriate use of the FBI information. The Attorney General and Secretary of State, in consultation with the Secretary of the Treasury, must report within 18 months of enactment and every two years thereafter on development, implementation, efficacy and privacy implications of the process. Sections 405 and 1008, discussed below, call for studies and reports to Congress on the feasibility of related enhancements in the systems to which this section gives access.

Section 404. Limited Authority to Pay Overtime.

In more normal times, Justice Department appropriations legislation placed a $30,000 cap on the amount of overtime that could paid individual INS officers. In light of the extraordinary circumstances at the end of the last fiscal year, section 404 repeals the limitation contained in the INS appropriation for border services for fiscal year 2001, 114 Stat. 2762-58 to 2762A-59 (2000).

Section 405. Report on the Integrated Automated Fingerprint Identification System for Ports of Entry and Overseas Consular Posts.

Section 405 directs the Attorney General, after consultation with the Secretaries of State, the Treasury, and Transportation, as well as other appropriate agency heads, to study and report upon the feasibility of enhancing the FBI's Integrated Automated Fingerprint Identification System (IAFIS) and other identification systems in order to better screen applications seeking to enter this country. The section authorizes appropriations of $2 million to the purpose.

Subtitle B – Enhanced Immigration Provisions

Section 411. Definitions Relating to Terrorism.

Foreign nationals (aliens) are deportable from the United States if they were inadmissible at the time they entered the country or if they have subsequently engaged in terrorist activity, 8 U.S.C. 1227(a)(1)(A),(a)(4)(B), 1182(a)(3)(B)(iv). Aliens may be inadmissible for any number of terrorism-related reasons, 8 U.S.C. 1182(a)(3)(B).

Section 411 adds to the terrorism-related grounds upon which an alien may be denied admission into the United States.

Prior law recognized five categories of terrorism-related factors which rendered an alien inadmissible. Section 411 redefines two of these, engaging in terrorist activity and representing a terrorist organization, 8 U.S.C. 1182(a)(3)(B)(iv), (a)(3)(B)(i)(IV), and it adds three more, espousing terrorist activity, being the spouse or child of an inadmissible alien, associating with a terrorist organization and intending to engage in activities that could endanger the welfare, safety or security of the United States, 8 U.S.C. 1182(a)(3)(B)(i)(VI), (a)(3)(B)(i)(VII), 1182(a)(3)(F).

Earlier law defined engaging in terrorist activity, which is grounds for both inadmissibility and deportation, to encompass soliciting on behalf of a terrorist organization or providing material support to a terrorist organization, 8 U.S.C. 1182(a)(3)(B)(iii)(2000 ed.). It did not explain in so many words, however, what constituted a "terrorist organization," although it presumably at the very least included groups designated a terrorist organizations under section 219 of the Immigration and Nationality Act (8 U.S.C. 1189). Although only effective after designation, §411(c), section 411 defines "terrorist organization" to include not only organizations designated under section 219 but also organizations which the Secretary has identified in the *Federal Register* as having provided material support for, committed, incited, planned, or gathered information on potential targets of, terrorist acts of violence, 8 U.S.C. 1182(a)(3)(B)(vi), (a)(3)(B)(iv). It then recasts the definition of engaging in terrorist activities to include solicitation on behalf of such organizations, or recruiting on their behalf, or providing them with material support, 8 U.S.C. 1182(a)(3)(B)(iv). Nevertheless, section 411 permits the Secretary of State or Attorney General to conclude that the material support prohibition does not apply to particular aliens, 8 U.S.C. 1182(a)(3)(B)(vi).

Prior law made representatives of terrorist organizations designated by the Secretary under section 219 (8 U.S.C. 1189) inadmissible, 8 U.S.C. 1182(a)(3)(B)(i) (IV)(2000 ed.). And so they remain. Section 411 makes representatives of political, social or similar groups, whose public endorsements of terrorist activities undermines our efforts to reduce or eliminate terrorism, inadmissible as well, 8 U.S.C. 1882(a)(3) (B)(i)(IV).

An individual who uses his or her place of prominence to endorse, espouse, or advocate support for terrorist activities or terrorist organizations in a manner which the Secretary of State concludes undermines our efforts to reduce or eliminate terrorism becomes inadmissible under section 411, 8 U.S.C. 1182(a)(3)(B)(i)(VI).

The spouse or child of an alien, who is inadmissible on terrorist grounds for activity occurring within the last 5 years, is likewise inadmissible, unless the child or spouse was reasonably unaware of the disqualify conduct or has repudiated the disqualify conduct, 8 U.S.C. 1182(a)(3)(B)(i)(VII), 1182(a)(3)(B)(ii).

Finally, any alien, whom the Secretary of State or the Attorney General conclude has associated with a terrorist organization and intends to engage in conduct dangerous to the welfare, safety, security of the United States while in their country, is inadmissible, 8 U.S.C. 1182(a)(3)(F).

Section 219 of the Immigration and Nationality Act (8 U.S.C. 1189) permits the Secretary to designate as terrorist organizations any foreign group which he finds to have engaged in terrorist activities. A second subsection 411(c) permits him to designate groups which as subnational groups or clandestine agents, engage in "premeditated, politically motivated violence perpetrated against noncombatant targets," or groups which retain the capacity and intent to engage in terrorism or terrorist activity, 8 U.S.C. 1189(a)(1)(B).

Section 412. Mandatory Detention of Suspected Terrorists; Habeas Corpus; Judicial Review.

Section 412 permits the Attorney General to detain alien terrorist suspects for up to seven days, 8 U.S.C. 1226a. He must certify that he has reasonable grounds to believe that the suspects either are engaged in conduct which threatens the national security of the United States or are inadmissible or deportable on grounds of terrorism, espionage, sabotage, or sedition. Within seven days, the Attorney General must initiate removal or criminal proceedings or release the alien. If the alien is held, the determination must be reexamined every six months to confirm that the alien's release would threaten national security or endanger some individual or the general public. The Attorney General's determinations are subject to review only under writs of habeas corpus issued out of any federal district court but appealable only to the United States Court of Appeals for the District Columbia. The Attorney General must report to the Judiciary Committee on the details of the operation of section 412.

Uncertain is the relationship between section 412 and the President's Military Order of November 13, 2001, which allows the Secretary of Defense to detain designated alien terrorist suspects, within the United States or elsewhere, without express limitation or condition except with regard to food, water, shelter, clothing, medical treatment, religious exercise, and a proscription on invidious discrimination, 66 *Fed.Reg.* 57833, 57834 (Nov. 16, 2001).

Section 413. Multilateral Cooperation Against Terrorists.

State Department records concerning its processing of visa applications are confidential and generally available only for court and law enforcement purposes, 8 U.S.C. 1202(f). Section 413 authorizes the Secretary of State to share the information with other countries in order to combat terrorism, drug trafficking, gun running, smuggling of immigrants, or other criminal activity, either on a case by case basis or pursuant to a general agreement.

Section 414. Visa Integrity and Security.

The Illegal Immigration Reform and Immigrant Responsibility Act of 1996, 8 U.S.C. 1365a, instructed the Attorney General to implement an integrated entry and exit data system for airports, seaports and land border ports of entry. Section 414 expresses the sense of Congress that he should do so expeditiously and authorizes such appropriations as are necessary.

The section also directs the Attorney General and the Secretary of State to focus particularly on the use of biometric technology and tamper-resistant documents readable at ports of entry and to see to the development of a system that can be used by federal law enforcement officers to identify and detain individuals who pose a threat to U.S. national security.

Finally, it calls for the Office of Home Land Security to report to the Congress within a year of the enactment on the information needed for federal authorities to identify those seeking to enter the United States who are associated with terrorists organizations or otherwise pose a threat to our national security.

Section 415. Participation of Office of Homeland Security on Entry-Exit Task Force.

Section 415 adds the Office of Home Land Security to the Integrated Entry and Exit Data System Task Force, 8 U.S.C. 1365a note.

Section 416. Foreign Student Monitoring Program.

Section 417 authorizes appropriations of $36.8 million for the period ending on January 1, 2003 to implement and expand the program for collection of information relating to nonimmigrant foreign students and other exchange program participants, 8 U.S.C. 1372. The section adds air flight schools, language training schools, and vocations schools to the list of institutions whose students are to be included in the reporting requirement.

Section 417. Machine Readable Passports.

Section 217 of the Immigration and Nationality Act permits a visa waiver program with respect to foreign tourists from countries which among things issue machine-readable passports that comply with international standards (or anticipate being able to do so prior to October 1, 2003), 8 U.S.C. 1187(c). Section 417 directs the Secretary of State to report the results of annual audits of the progress of program countries towards full implementation of machine-readable passport capability, of the existence of programs to prevent passport theft and counterfeiting, and of the development of tamper-proof passports. Subject to a progress waiver by the Secretary of State, the section limits the countries eligible for visa waiver program participation to those who have machine-readable passports as of October 1, 2003 (rather than October 1, 2007 as was previously the case).

Section 418. Prevention of Consulate Shopping.

Section 418 commands the Secretary of State to determine whether consular shopping is a problem, to take steps to remedy any such problem, and to report to Congress on the action taken.

Subtitle C – Preservation of Immigration Benefits for Victims of Terrorism

The House Committee on the Judiciary explained a similar subtitle by noting that, "It is certain that some aliens fell victim to the terrorist attacks on the U.S. on September 11. This subtitle endeavors to modify immigration law to provide humanitarian relief to these victims and their family members," H.Rept. 107-236, at 66. Since the subtitle in the USA PATRIOT Act is largely unchanged from the subtitle reported out by the House Committee on the Judiciary, the analysis that follows is largely that of the Committee.

Section 421. Special Immigration Status.

"The [USA PATRIOT] Act provides permanent resident status through the special immigrant program to an alien who was the beneficiary of a petition filed (on or before September 11) to grant the alien permanent residence as an employer-sponsored immigrant or of an application for labor certification (filed on or before September 11), if the petition or application was rendered null because of the disability of the beneficiary or loss of employment of the beneficiary due to physical damage to, or destruction of, the business of the petitioner or applicant as a direct result of the terrorist attacks on September 11, or because of the death of the petitioner or applicant as a direct result of the terrorist attacks. Permanent residence would be granted to an alien who was the spouse or child of an alien who was the beneficiary of a petition filed on or before September 11 to grant the beneficiary permanent residence as a family-sponsored immigrant (as long as the spouse or child follows to join not later than September 11, 2003). Permanent residence would be granted to the beneficiary of a petition for a nonimmigrant visa as the spouse or the fiancé (and their children) of a U.S. citizen where the petitioning citizen died as a direct result of the terrorist attack. The section also provides permanent resident status to the grandparents of a child both of whose parents died as a result of the terrorist attacks, if either of such deceased parents was a citizen of the U.S. or a permanent resident," H.Rept. 107-236, at 66-7 (2001).

Section 422. Extension of Filing or Reentry Deadlines.

"The Act provides that an alien who was legally in a nonimmigrant status and was disabled as a direct result of the terrorist attacks on September 11 (and his or her spouse and children) may remain lawfully in the U.S. (and receive work authorization) until the later of the date that his or her status normally terminates or September 11, 2002. Such status is also provided to the nonimmigrant spouse and children of an alien who died as a direct result of the terrorist attacks.

Where an alien was prevented from taking timely action because of office closures, airline schedule disruptions or other similar impediments, the "Act provides that an alien who was lawfully present as a nonimmigrant at the time of the terrorist attacks will be granted 60 additional days to file an application for extension or change of status if the alien was prevented from so filing as a direct result of the terrorist attacks. Also, an alien who was lawfully present as a nonimmigrant at the time of the attacks but was then unable to timely depart the U.S. as a direct result of the attacks will be considered to have departed legally if doing so before November 11. An alien who was in lawful nonimmigrant status at the time of the attacks (and his or her spouse and children) but not in the U.S. at that time and was then prevented from returning to the U.S. in order to file a timely application for an extension of status as a direct result of the terrorist attacks will be given 60 additional days to file an application and will have his or her status extended 60 days beyond the original due date   of   the   application.

"Under current law, winners of the fiscal year 2001 diversity visa lottery must enter the U.S. or adjust status by September 30, 2001. The Act provides that such an alien may enter the U.S. or adjust status until April 1, 2002, if the alien was prevented from doing so by September 30, 2001 as a direct result of the terrorist attacks. If the visa quota for the 2001 diversity visa program has already been exceeded, the alien shall be counted under the 2002 program. Also, if a winner of the 2001 lottery died as a direct result of the terrorist attacks, the spouse and children of the alien shall still be eligible for permanent residence under the program. The ceiling placed on the number of diversity immigrants shall not be exceeded in any case.

"Under the Act, in the case of an alien who was issued an immigrant visa that expires before December 31, 2001, if the alien was unable to timely enter the U.S. as a direct result of the terrorist attacks, the validity shall be extended until December 31.

"Under the Act, in the case of an alien who was granted parole that expired on or after September 11, if the alien was unable to enter the U.S. prior to the expiration date as a direct result of the terrorist attacks, the parole is extended an additional 90 days.

"Under the Act, in the case of an alien granted voluntary departure that expired between September 11 and October 11, 2001, voluntary departure is extended an additional 30 days," H.Rept. 107-236, at 67-8 (2001).

Section 423. Humanitarian Relief or Certain Surviving Spouses and Children.

"Current law provides that an alien who was the spouse of a U.S. citizen for at least 2 years before the citizen died shall remain eligible for immigrant status as an immediate relative. This also applies to the children of the alien. The Act provides that if the citizen died as a direct result of the terrorist attacks, the 2 year requirement is waived.

"The Act provides that if an alien spouse, child, or unmarried adult son or daughter had been the beneficiary of an immigrant visa petition filed by a permanent resident who died as a direct result of the terrorist attacks, the alien will still be eligible for permanent residence. In addition, if an alien spouse, child, or unmarried adult son or daughter of a permanent resident who died as a direct result of the terrorist attacks was present in the U.S. on September 11 but had not yet been petitioned for permanent residence, the alien can self-petition for permanent residence.

"The Act provides that an alien spouse or child of an alien who 1) died as a direct result of the terrorist attacks and 2) was a permanent resident (petitioned-for by an employer) or an applicant for adjustment of status for an employment-based immigrant visa, may have his or her application for adjustment adjudicated despite the death (if the application was filed prior to the death)," H.Rept. 107-236, at 68 (2001).

Section 424. "Age-out" Protection for Children.

"Under current law, certain visas are only available to an alien until the alien's 21st birthday. The Act provides that an alien whose 21st birthday occurs this September and who is a beneficiary for a petition or application filed on or before September 11 shall be considered to remain a child for 90 days after the alien's 21st birthday. For an alien whose 21st birthday occurs after this September, (and who had a petition for application filed on his or her behalf on or before September 11) the alien shall be considered to remain a child for 45 days after the alien's 21st birthday," H.Rept. 107-236, at 68 (2001).

Section 425. Temporary Administrative Relief.

"The Act provides that temporary administrative relief may be provided to an alien who was lawfully present on September 10, was on that date the spouse, parent or child of someone who died or was disabled as a direct result of the terrorist attacks, and is not otherwise entitled to relief under any other provision of Subtitle [C]," H.Rept. 107-236, at 68 (2001).

Section 426. Evidence of Death, Disability, or Loss of Employment.

"The Attorney General shall establish appropriate standards for evidence demonstrating that a death, disability, or loss of employment due to physical damage to, or destruction of, a business, occurred as a direct result of the terrorist attacks on September 11. The Attorney General is not required to promulgate regulations prior to implementing Subtitle [C]," H.Rept. 107-326, at 68-9 (2001).

Section 427. No Benefits to Terrorists or Family Members of Terrorists.

"No benefit under Subtitle B shall be provided to anyone culpable for the terrorist attacks on September 11 or to any family member of such an individual," H.Rept. 107-236, at 69 (2001).

Section 428. Definitions.

"The term 'specified terrorist activity' means any terrorist activity conducted against the Government or the people of the U.S. on September 11, 2001," H.Rept. 107-236, at 69 (2001).

Title V – Removing Obstacles to Investigating Terrorism

Section 501. Attorney General's Authority to Pay Rewards to Combat Terrorism.

The Attorney General enjoys the power to pay rewards in criminal cases, but his power under other authorities is often subject to caps on the amount he might pay. Thus as a general rule, he may award amounts up to $25,000 for the capture of federal offenders, 18 U.S.C. 3059, and may pay rewards in any amount in recognition of assistance to the Department of Justices as long as the Appropriations and Judiciary Committees are notified of any rewards in excess of $100,000, 18 U.S.C. 3059B. Although he has special reward authority in terrorism cases, individual awards are capped at $500,000, (the ceiling for the total amount paid in such rewards is $5 million), and rewards of $100,000 or more require his personal approval or that of the President, 18 U.S.C. 3071-3077. Over the last several years, annual appropriation acts have raised the $500,000 cap to $2 million and the $5 million ceiling to $10 million, *e.g.*, Public Law 106-553, 114 Stat. 2762-67 (2000); Public Law 106-113, 113 Stat. 1501A-19 (1999); Public Law105-277, 112 Stat. 2681-66 (1998).

The USA PATRIOT Act supplies the Attorney General with the power to pay rewards to combat terrorism in any amount and without an aggregate limitation, but for rewards of $250,000 or more it insists on personal approval of the Attorney General or the President and on notification of the Appropriations and Judiciary Committees, §501. The funds to pay the rewards may come from any federal department or agency. In addition, the counterterrorism fund of section 101 can be used "without limitation" to pay rewards to prevent, investigate, or prosecute terrorism.

Section 502. Secretary of State's Authority to Pay Rewards.

The Secretary of State's reward authority was already somewhat more generous than that of the Attorney General. He may pay rewards of up to $5 million for information in international terrorism cases as long as he personally approves payments in excess of $100,000, 22 U.S.C. 2708. The Act removes the $5 million cap and allows rewards to be paid for information concerning the whereabouts of terrorist leaders and facilitating the dissolution of terrorist organizations, §502.

Section 503. DNA Identification of Terrorists and Other Violent Offenders.

Federal law allows the Attorney General to collect DNA samples from federal prisoners convicted of a variety of violent crimes, 42 U.S.C. 14135a(d)(2). Section 503 expands the range. It permits samples to be taken from any federal prisoner convicted of a federal crime of terrorism (as defined in 18 U.S.C. 2332b(g)(5)(B)), or a crime of violence (as defined by 18 U.S.C. 16), or attempt or conspiracy to commit a crime of terrorism or violence.

Section 504. Coordination With Law Enforcement.

Federal intelligence officers who wish to conduct electronic surveillance or physical searches under a FISA court order must certify that the acquisition of foreign intelligence information constitutes a significant purpose for the surveillance or search, 50 U.S.C. 1805(a)(7)(B), 1823(a)(7)(B). Section 504 confirms that the certification requirement does not preclude intelligence officers operating under FISA orders from coordinating their investigations with law enforcement officers in cases involving a foreign attack or other grave hostile attack, sabotage or international terrorism by a foreign power or agent, or foreign clandestine intelligence activities.

Section 505. Miscellaneous National Security Authorities.

Three statutes, the Electronic Privacy Act, the Right to Financial Privacy Act, and Fair Credit Reporting Act, authorize third parties to release confidential communication transaction records, financial reports, and credit information for intelligence purposes upon the written request of senior FBI officials. Prior to section 505, the FBI was required to assert that the information sought was related to a foreign power, foreign agent, an international terrorist, or an individual engaged in clandestine intelligence activities, 18 U.S.C. 2709(b)(2), 12 U.S.C. 3414(a)(5), 15 U.S.C. 1681u. In an explanation that applies to all three statutory provisions, the House Committee on the Judiciary described the change made in the Electronic Privacy Act section: "Section 2709 of title 18 permits the Director of the Federal Bureau of Investigation to request, through a National Security Letter (NSL), subscriber information and toll billing records of a wire or electronic communication service provider. The request must certify (1) that the information sought is relevant to an authorized foreign counterintelligence investigation; and (2) there are specific and articulable facts that the person or entity to whom the information sought pertains is a foreign power or an agent of a foreign power as defined in FISA. This requirement is more burdensome than the corresponding criminal authorities, which require only a certification of relevance. The additional requirement of documentation of specific and articulable facts showing the person or entity is a foreign power or an agent of a foreign power cause substantial delays in counterintelligence and counterterrorism investigations. Such delays are unacceptable as our law enforcement and intelligence community works to thwart additional terrorist attacks that threaten the national security of the United States and her citizens' lives and livelihoods.

"Section [505] amends title 18 U.S.C. 2709 to mirror criminal subpoenas and allow a NSL to be issued when the FBI certifies, the information sought is 'relevant to an authorized foreign counterintelligence investigation,'" H.Rept. 107-236, at 61-2 (2001).

Section 506. Extension of Secret Service Jurisdiction.

The federal computer fraud and abuse section, 18 U.S.C. 1030, originally vested the Secret Service with investigative jurisdiction over violations other than those dealing with classified information under 18 U.S.C. 1030(a)(1). The Secret Service also enjoyed investigative authority over offenses involving credit and debit card frauds as well as offenses involving false identification documents or devices, 18 U.S.C.3056(b)(3)(2000 ed.).

Section 506 preserves the Service's jurisdiction with respect to section 1030. It explicitly notes the FBI's investigative jurisdiction over offenses under paragraph 1030(a)(1) and the FBI's concurrent jurisdiction over offenses under the remainder of 18 U.S.C. 1030. The section amends paragraph 3056(b)(3) to enlarge the Service's jurisdiction from offenses involving "credit and debit card frauds, and false identification documents and devices" to crimes involving "access device fraud, false identification documents or devices, *and any fraud or other criminal or unlawful activity in or against any federally insured financial institution.*"

Section 507. Disclosure of Educational Records.

Section 507 calls for an ex parte court order procedure under which senior Justice Department officials may seek authorization to collect educational records relevant to an investigation or prosecution of a crime of terrorism (as an exception to the confidentiality requirements of the General Education Provisions Act, 20 U.S.C. 1232g). Educational institutions who comply receive immunity from liability for the disclosure.

Section 508. Disclosure of Information From NCES Surveys.

Section 508 creates a similar ex parte court order procedure under which senior Justice Department officials may seek authorization to collect individually identifiable information from the National Center for Education (as an exception to the confidentiality requirements of the National Education Statistics Act, 20 U.S.C. 9007). Officers and employees of the Center who cooperate receive immunity from liability for the disclosure.

Title VI – Providing for Victims of Terrorism, Public Safety Officers, and Their Families

Subtitle A – Aid to Families of Public Safety Officers

Section 611. Expedited Payment for Public Safety Officers Involved in the Prevention, Investigation, Rescue, or Recovery Efforts Related to a Terrorist Attack.

Federal law authorizes benefits for those victimized by the death or catastrophic injury resulting in permanent and total disability of a public safety officer in the line of duty, subject to certain limitation, 42 U.S.C. 3796 *et seq.* Gross negligence, substantial contributory negligence, and employment other than in a civilian capacity are among the disqualifying factors, 42 U.S.C. 3796a, and there is a $5 million cap on benefits awarded in any fiscal year, 42 U.S.C. 3796. In cases of death or catastrophic injury sustained in the line of duty in relation to a terrorist attack, section 611 waives the cap and these disqualifications and orders the Bureau of Justice Assistance, which administers the program, to make payments within 30 days of receipt of a public agency's certification of eligibility in a particular case.

Section 612. Technical Correction With Respect to Expedited Payments for Heroic Public Safety Officers.

Public Law 107-37, 115 Stat. 219 (2001), makes the same adjustments as those of section 611 for death and catastrophic injuries sustained in the line of duty in the course of rescue or recovery efforts related to the terrorist attacks of September 11. Section 612 confirms certain technical corrections made by the clerk and that the Public Law extends to death and catastrophic injuries producing permanent and total disability.

Section 613. Public Safety Officers Benefit Program Payment Increases.

Section 613 raises the amount of the benefit from $100,000 to $250,000, effective January 1, 2001, 42 U.S.C. 3796.

Section 614. Office of Justice Programs.

Title I of the Omnibus Crime Control and Safe Streets Act (Pubic Law 90-351), as amended, creates the Office of Justice Programs (OJP) and a series of federal criminal justice and related assistance programs administered under its auspices, 42 U.S.C. 3711 *et seq.* In 1998, while Congress was considering reauthorization of some of those programs, it authorized the Office of Justice Programs to exercise authority over and approve grants, contracts and the like with respect to it's programs during fiscal year 1999, Public Law 105-277, 112 Stat. 2681-67 (1998). The following year, it renewed that authority for fiscal year 2000, but denied OJP authority to approve grants under the National Institute of Justice, the Bureau of Justice Statistics, and a few Juvenile Justice and Delinquency Prevention programs, Public Law 106-113, 113 Stat. 1501A-20 (1999). The fiscal year 2001 appropriations act carried forward by cross reference the same provisions with the same limitations, Public Law 106-553, 114 Stat. 2762A-67 (2000). Section 614 removes the limitations.

Subtitle B – Amendments to the Victims of Crime Act of 1984

Section 621. Crime Victims Fund.

The Crime Victims Fund receives most of the fines collected for violations of federal criminal law and distributes them for purposes of victim assistance and compensation, 42 U.S.C. 10601-10604. Section 621 authorizes the Fund to receive gifts from private individuals. It instructs the Department of Justice, which administers the Fund, to distribute every fiscal year between 90 and 110% of the amount distributed in the previous year (120% in any year when the amount on hand is twice the amount distributed the previous year).

Pre-existing law allocated 48.5% of the amounts available under the Fund to crime victim compensation grants, 48.5% to crime victim assistance grants, and 3% to discretionary grants, 42 U.S.C. 10601(d)(4)(2000 ed.). Section 621 reduces the amounts available for compensation and assistance grants by 1% and increases to 5% the amount available for discretionary grants.

The section allows the Department of Justice to establish a $50 million antiterrorism emergency reserve for supplemental grants to compensate and assist victims of terrorism or mass violence. It also removes the otherwise applicable caps on the amounts transferred to the Fund in response to the terrorist acts of September 11.

Section 622. Crime Victim Compensation.

Before passage of section 622, individual victim compensation program grants were capped at 40% of the amount awarded in the previous year. Section 622 lifts the cap to 60% beginning in fiscal year 2003.

It also (1) removes the requirement that an eligible state crime victim compensation program provide compensation to state residents for terrorist crimes committed overseas, 42 U.S.C. 10602(b)(6)(B); (2) drops crimes involving terrorism from the definition of "compensable crimes," 42 U.S.C. 10602(d)(3); (3) provides that unlike other victim compensation, victim compensation received under Title IV of the Air Transportation Safety and System Stabilization Act (September 11 Victim Compensation Fund), Public Law 107-42, 115 Stat. 237, 49 U.S.C. 40101 note, may be considered income, a resource, or an asset for purposes of qualifying as an indigent for any federal or federal supported grant or benefit program, 42 U.S.C. 10602(c); (4) adds Title IV victim compensation to the "double dipping" restriction that applies to victim compensation programs, 42 U.S.C. 10602(e); and (5) allows the Virgin Islands to participate as a state in the victim compensation grant program, 42 U.S.C. 10602(d)(4).

Section 623. Crime Victim Assistance.

Section 623 expands the crime victim assistance grant program to permit grants to federal agencies who perform local law enforcement functions in or on behalf of the District of Columbia, the Virgin Islands, or any other U.S. territory or possessions. It prohibits program discrimination against crime victims based on their disagreement with the manner in which the state is prosecuting the underlying offense, 42 U.S.C.10603(b)(1)(F); allows grants to be used for program evaluation and compliance efforts, 42 U.S.C. 10603(c)(1)(A); for fellowships, clinical internships, and training programs, 42 U.S.C. 10603(c)(3)(E). Finally, it reverses the preference for victim service grants over demonstration projects and training grants, so that not more than 50% of the amounts available for crime victim assistance grants shall be used for victim service grants and not less than 50% for demonstration projects and training grants, 42 U.S.C. 10603(c)(2).

Section 624. Victims of Terrorism.

Title VIII of the Omnibus Diplomatic Security and Antiterrorism Act of 1986, Public Law 99-399, 100 Stat. 879 (1986), provides victims' benefits for the Iranian hostages, 5 U.S.C. 5569. The Antiterrorism and Effective Death Penalty Act, Public Law 104-132, 110 Stat. 1243, 42 U.S.C. 10603b, and the Victims of Trafficking and Violence Protection Act of 2000, Public Law 106-386, 114 Stat. 1545, 42 U.S.C. 10603c, establish compensation programs for victims of terrorism or mass destruction and victims of international terrorism respectively.

Prior to the enactment of section 624 only the states were eligible for compensation and assistance grants on behalf of the victims of terrorism or mass destruction occurring within the United States, and victims eligible for benefits under the diplomatic security law were ineligible for compensation and assistance under the general provisions covering victims of terrorism or mass destruction occurring abroad, 42 U.S.C. 10603b(2000 ed.). Section 624 removes the diplomatic security law disqualification and permits grants to victim service organizations – federal, state, local and nongovernmental agencies – to provide emergency victim relief, 42 U.S.C. 10603b.

Further, the section reduces the amount of compensation available to victims of international terrorism generally by any amount a victim has received under the diplomatic security law, 42 U.S.C. 10603c.

Title VII – Increased Information Sharing for Critical Infrastructure Protection

Section 701. Expansion of Regional Information Sharing Systems to Facilitate Federal-State-Local Law Enforcement Response Related to Terrorist Attacks.

The Office of Justice Programs is authorized to make grants and enter into contracts with state and local law enforcement agencies and with nonprofit organizations to identify and combat multi-jurisdictional criminal conspiracies, 42 U.S.C. 3796h. Section 701 amends section 3796h to authorize appropriations of $50 million for fiscal year 2002 and $100 million for fiscal year 2003 to be used to establish and operate a secure information sharing system to combat multi-jurisdictional terrorist conspiracies and activities.

Title VIII – Strengthening the Criminal Laws Against Terrorism

Section 801. Terrorist Attacks and Other Acts of Violence Against Mass Transportation Systems.

Pre-existing federal law criminalized, among other things, wrecking trains, 18 U.S.C. 1992; damaging commercial motor vehicles or their facilities, 18 U.S.C. 33, or threatening to do so, 18 U.S.C. 35; destroying vessels within the navigable waters of the United States, 18 U.S.C. 2273; destruction of vehicles or other property used in activities affecting interstate or foreign commerce by fire or explosives, 18 U.S.C. 844(i); possession of a biological agent or toxin as a weapon or a threat, attempt, or conspiracy to do so, 18 U.S.C. 175; use of a weapon of mass destruction affecting interstate or foreign commerce or a threat, attempt, or conspiracy to do so, 18 U.S.C. 2332a; commission of a federal crime of violence while armed with a firearm, or of federal felony while in possession an explosive, 18 U.S.C. 924(c), 844(h); and conspiracy to commit a federal crime, 18 U.S.C. 371.

Section 801 fills in some of the gaps in these proscriptions. It makes terrorist attacks and other acts of violence against mass transportation systems federal crimes, punishable by imprisonment for any term of years or life if the conveyance is occupied at the time of the offense, and imprisonment for not more than twenty years in other cases. Under its provisions, it is a crime to willfully

- wreck, derail, burn, or disable mass transit;

- place a biological agent or destructive device on mass transit recklessly or with the intent to endanger;
- burn or place a biological agent or destructive device in or near a mass transit facility knowing a conveyance is likely to be disabled;
- impair a mass transit signal system;
- interfere with a mass transit dispatcher, operator, or maintenance personnel in the performance of their duties recklessly or with the intent to endanger;
- act with the intent to kill or seriously injure someone on mass transit property;
- convey a false alarm concerning violations of the section;
- attempt to violate the section;
- threaten or conspire to violate the section

when the violation involves interstate travel, communication, or transportation of materials or that involves a carrier engaged in or affecting interstate or foreign commerce, 18 U.S.C. 1993.

Section 802. Definition of Domestic Terrorism.

Section 802 adjusts the definition of international terrorism in 18 U.S.C. 2331 and borrows from it to define domestic terrorism. Section 2331 has for some time defined international terrorism as those criminal acts of violence, committed primarily overseas or internationally, that appear to be intended to intimidate or coerce a civilian population, or to influence a governmental policy by intimidation or coercion, or to affect the conduct of a government by assassination or kidnaping, 18 U.S.C. 2331(1). Section 802 simply modifies this last element to include acts that appear to be intended to affect the conduct of a government by *mass destruction*, assassination or kidnaping.

It defines domestic terrorism as those criminal acts dangerous to human life, committed primarily within the United States, that appear to be intended to intimidate or coerce a civilian population, or to influence a governmental policy by intimidation or coercion, or to affect the conduct of a government by mass destruction, assassination or kidnaping, 18 U.S.C. 2331(5).

Section 803. Prohibition Against Harboring Terrorists.

It is a federal crime to harbor aliens, 8 U.S.C. 1324, or those engaged in espionage, 18 U.S.C. 792, or to commit misprision of a felony (which may take the form of harboring the felon), 18 U.S.C. 4, or to act as an accessory after the fact to a federal crime (including by harboring the offender), 18 U.S.C. 3. The Justice Department asked that a terrorist harboring offense be added to the espionage section, and that it be given extraterritorial effect and venue flexibility.

Section 803 instead establishes a separate offense which punishes harboring terrorists by imprisonment for not more than ten years and/or a fine of not more than $250,000, 18 U.S.C. 2339. The predicate offense list consists of:

! destruction of aircraft or their facilities, 18 U.S.C. 32;
! biological weapons offenses, 18 U.S.C. 175;
! chemical weapons offenses, 18 U.S.C. 229;

! nuclear weapons offenses, 18 U.S.C. 831;

! bombing federal buildings, 18 U.S.C. 844(f);

! destruction of an energy facility, 18 U.S.C. 1366;

! violence committed against maritime navigational facilities, 18 U.S.C. 2280;

! offenses involving weapons of mass destruction, 18 U.S.C. 2232a;

! international terrorism, 18 U.S.C. 2232b;

! sabotage of a nuclear facility, 42 U.S.C. 2284;

! air piracy, 49 U.S.C. 46502.

It permits prosecution either at the place the harboring occurred or where the underlying act of terrorism committed by the sheltered terrorist might be prosecuted. In order to enjoy the full benefits of section 803, the prosecution may have to establish a nexus between the act of terrorism and the site of concealment, *U.S.Const. Art.III*, §2, cl.3; *Amend. IV*; *United States v. Cabrales*, 524 U.S. 1 (1998). On the other hand, if the acts of terrorism occur in the United States or over which the United States has jurisdiction, the crime of harboring the terrorist even overseas can be prosecuted in the United States in all likelihood without amending existing law, *cf.*, *United States v. Felix-Gutierrez*, 940 F.2d 1200, 1205 (9th Cir. 1991)("crime of accessory after the fact gives rise to extraterritorial jurisdiction to the same extent as the underlying offense").

Section 804. Jurisdiction Over Crimes Committed at U.S. Facilities Abroad.

Crime is usually outlawed, prosecuted and punished where it is committed. In the case of the United States, this a matter of practical and diplomatic preference rather than constitutional necessity. Consequently, a surprising number of federal criminal laws have extraterritorial application. In some instances, the statute proscribing the misconduct expressly permits the exercise of extraterritorial jurisdiction, *e.g.*, 18 U.S.C. 2332a (relating to use of weapons of mass destruction by an American overseas). In others, such as those banning assassination of Members of Congress, 18 U.S.C. 351, or the attempted murder of federal law enforcement officers, 18 U.S.C. 1114, the court will assume Congress intended the prohibitions to have extraterritorial reach.[10]

Section 804 touches upon extraterritoriality only to a limited extent and in somewhat unusual manner. The special maritime and territorial jurisdiction of the United States represent two variations of the extraterritorial jurisdiction. Congress has made most common law crimes – murder, sexual abuse, kidnaping, assault, robbery, theft and the like – federal crimes when committed within the special maritime and territorial jurisdiction of the United States.

The special maritime jurisdiction of the United States extends to the vessels of the United States. Historically, the territorial jurisdiction of the United States was thought to reach those areas over which Congress enjoyed state-like legislative

---

[10] *United Stats v. Layton*, 855 F.2d 1388 (9th Cir. 1981); *United States v. Benitez*, 741 F.2d 1312 (11th Cir. 1984) *United States v. Bowman*, 260 U.S. 94 (1922); *Ford v. United States*, 273 U.S. 593 (1927).

jurisdiction. For some time, those territories were located exclusively within the confines of the United States, but over the years came to include at least temporarily, Hawaii, the Philippines, and other American overseas territories and possessions. Recently, the lower federal courts have become divided over the question of whether laws enacted to apply within federal enclaves within the United States and American territories overseas might also apply to areas overseas over which the United States has proprietary control, *compare, United States v. Gatlin*, 216 F.3d 207 (2d Cir. 2000); *United States v. Laden*, 92 F.Supp.2d 189 (S.D.N.Y. 2000); *with, United States v. Corey*, 232 F.3d 1166 (9th Cir. 2000); *United States v. Erdos*, 474 F.2d 157 (4th Cir. 1973). The section resolves the conflict by declaring within the territorial jurisdiction of the United States includes those overseas areas used by American governmental entities for their activities or residences for their personnel, at least to the extent that crimes are committed by or against an American. It is intended as a residual provision and therefore does not apply where it would conflict with a treaty obligation or where the offender is covered by the Military Extraterritorial Jurisdiction Act (18 U.S.C. 3261).

Section 805. Material Support of Terrorism.

Sections 2339A and 2339B of title 18 of the United States Code ban providing material support to individuals and to organizations that commit various crimes of terrorism. Section 804 amends the sections in several ways, some at the behest of the Justice Department. Section 2339B (support of a terrorist organization) joins section 2339A (support of a terrorist) as a money laundering predicate offense, 18 U.S.C. 1956(c)(7)(D) The predicate offense list of 18 U.S.C. 2339A (support to terrorists) grows to include:

- ! chemical weapons offenses, 18 U.S.C. 229;
- ! terrorist attacks on mass transportation, 18 U.S.C. 1993 ;
- ! sabotage of a nuclear facility, 42 U.S.C. 2284; and
- ! sabotage of interstate pipelines, 49 U.S.C. 60123(b).

Section 805 also adds expert advice or assistance of the types of assistance that may not be provided under section 2339A. Prosecutions grounded on providing material assistance in the form of expert advice may encounter the same First Amendment vagueness problems some courts have found in assistance which takes the form of "training"and "personnel," *Humanitarian Law Project v. Reno*, 205 F.3d 1130, 1137-136 (9th Cir. 2000).

Finally, the section declares that a prosecution for violation of section 2339A (support of terrorists) may be brought where the support is provided or where the predicate act of terrorism occurs. The full benefit of this amendment may have to await clarification in the law concerning venue, *U.S.Const.* Art.III, §2, cl.3; Amend. IV; *United States v. Cabrales*, 524 U.S. 1 (1998).

Section 806. Assets of Foreign Terrorist Organizations.

Modern forfeiture law strips criminals of the proceeds and instruments of crime. Terrorism, however, neither produces profits of drug dealing nor requires the specialized equipment of the rum runner or the counterfeiter. Consequently, most forfeiture statutes do not reach the crimes of terrorism. Nevertheless terrorism, particularly international terrorism, requires financing; cash is the essential instrumentality of terrorism. The USA PATRIOT Act attacks terrorism at its most vulnerable spot, its need for financial support. The Act's invigorating of the International Economic Emergency Powers Act asset forfeiture and its money laundering measures are calculated to encumber and prevent terrorism by drying up its sources of financial support.

Section 806 supplies another tool for that effort. It subjects to civil forfeiture property wherever located: (1) which belongs to an individual or entity planning or engaging in domestic or international terrorism against the United States (as defined in 18 U.S.C. 2331) or which affords the individual a source of influence over a terrorist organization; (2) which is acquired or maintained for use in furtherance of acts of domestic or international terrorism committed against Americans; or (3) which is derived from or is useful for the commission of acts of domestic or international terrorism committed against the Americans, 18 U.S.C. 981(a)(1)(G). The section is something of a rarity in that it creates a forfeiture of estate (confiscation based solely on the property's relation to an offender rather than to the offense; discussed earlier with respect to section 106), traditionally thought to be at odds with the concept of civil in rem forfeiture and with the bans on corruption of the blood, *U.S.Const.* Art.III, §3, cl.2; Amend.V; *United States v. Grande,* 620 F.2d 1026 (4th Cir. 1980).

Section 807. Technical Clarification Relating to Provision of Material Support to Terrorism.

The Trade Sanctions Reform and Export Enhancement Act of 2000, Title IX of Public Law 106-387, 114 Stat. 1549A-69, limits the power of the President to unilaterally impose export restrictions on agricultural and medical products, subject to certain exceptions. Section 807 builds on the pronouncement of section 221(b)(2) to confirm that the trade sanctions bill should not be construed to limit or otherwise amend the prohibitions on providing material support to terrorist or terrorist organizations found in 18 U.S.C. 2339A and 2339B.

Section 808. Definition of Federal Crime of Terrorism.

Paragraph 2332b(g)(5)(b) lists a number of violent federal crimes within its definition of "federal crime[s] of terrorism" for purposes of the section's prohibition on acts of terrorism transcending national boundaries. Section 808 amends the definition for consistency with its use in various other sections of the USA PATRIOT Act. The Section drops a number of less serious crimes from the definition, such as simple assault (18 U.S.C. 351(e)), bomb scares (18 U.S.C. 844(e)), and malicious mischief (18 U.S.C. 1361), after reaffirming that the omitted offenses remain within the investigative jurisdiction of the Department of Justice. It places several more serious crimes within the definition, crimes like biological weapons offenses (18 U.S.C. 175b), cybercrime (18 U.S.C. 1030), terrorists attacks on mass transit (18 U.S.C. 1993), and various violent crimes committed aboard aircraft within U.S. jurisdiction (49 U.S.C. 46504, 46505(b)(3),(c), 46505).

Section 809. No Statute of Limitations for Certain Terrorism Offenses.

Prosecution for murder may be initiated at any time; there is no statute of limitations, 18 U.S.C. 3281. With a few exceptions, there is a five year statute of limitations on the prosecution of other federal crimes. Among the relevant exceptions before the USA PATRIOT Act was enacted, were an eight year statute of limitations for several terrorist offenses, 18 U.S.C. 3286,[11] and a ten year statute of limitations for arson in federal enclaves and explosives offenses involving federal property, property used in an activity affecting interstate commerce, and use of an explosive during the commission of a federal offense, 18 U.S.C. 3295. The Administration recommended the elimination of a statute of limitations in terrorism cases.

Section 809 takes a less dramatic approach. It eliminates the statute of limitations for any federal crime of terrorism (as defined by 18 U.S.C. 2332b(g)(5)(B), with the amendments of §808) that risks or results in a death or serious bodily injury, 18 U.S.C. 3286. In the absence of such a risk or result, all other terrorism offenses become subject to the eight year statute of limitations unless already covered by the ten year statute for explosives and arson offenses, 18 U.S.C. 3286 (§809).

Section 810. Alternative Maximum Penalties for Terrorism Offenses.

The Justice Department suggested an alternative term of imprisonment up to life imprisonment for anyone convicted of an offense designated a terrorist crime. It described the proposal as analogous to standard fine provisions of 18 U.S.C. 3571(b),(c), which in 1984 established a basic fine of $250,000 for any individual who committed a federal felony, notwithstanding the lower maximum fine described in the statute that outlawed the offense.

The proposal, however, failed to identify the critical elements that would trigger the alternative. Both practical and constitutional challenges might be thought to attend this failure to distinguish between those convicted of some "garden variety" crime of terrorism and the more serious offender meriting the alternative, supplementary penalty. Section 810 instead opts to simply increase the maximum penalties for various crimes of terrorism, particularly those which involve the taking of a human life and are not already capital offenses. It increases the maximum terms of imprisonment:

---

[11] 18 U.S.C. 32 (destruction of aircraft or aircraft facilities), 37 (violence at international airports), 112 (assaults on foreign dignitaries), 351 (crimes of violence against Members of Congress), 1116 (killing foreign dignitaries), 1203 (hostage taking), 1361 (destruction of federal property), 1751 (crimes of violence against the President), 2280 (violence against maritime navigation), 2281 (violence on maritime platforms), 2332 (terrorist violence against Americans overseas), 2332a (use of weapons of mass destruction), 2332b (acts of terrorism transcending national boundaries), 2340A (torture); 49 U.S.C. 46502 (air piracy), 46504 (interference with a flight crew), 46505 (carrying a weapon aboard an aircraft), and 46506 (assault, theft, robbery, sexual abuse, murder, manslaughter or attempted murder or manslaughter in the special aircraft jurisdiction of the United States).

❗ for life-threatening arson or arson of a dwelling committed within a federal enclave, from 20 years to any term of years or life, 18 U.S.C. 81;

❗ for causing more than $100,000 in damage to, or significantly impairing the operation of an energy facility, from 10 to 20 years (or any term of years or life, if death results), 18 U.S.C. 1366;

❗ for providing material support to a terrorist or a terrorist organization, from 10 to 15 years (or any term of years or life, if death results), 18 U.S.C. 2339A, 2339B;

❗ for destruction of national defense materials, from 10 to 20 years (or any term of years or life, if death results), 18 U.S.C. 2155;

❗ for sabotage of a nuclear facility, from 10 to 20 years (or any term of years or life, if death results), 42 U.S.C. 2284;

❗ for carrying a weapon or explosive aboard an aircraft within U.S. special aircraft jurisdiction, from 15 to 20 years (or any term of years or life, if death results), 49 U.S.C. 46505; and

❗ for sabotage of interstate gas pipeline facilities, from 15 to 20 years (or any term of years or life, if death results), 49 U.S.C. 60123.

Section 811. Penalties for Terrorist Conspiracies.

It is a separate federal offense punishable by imprisonment for not more than five years to conspire to commit any federal felony, 18 U.S.C. 371. Coconspirators are likewise subject to punishment for the underlying offense and for any other crimes committed in furtherance of the conspiracy. Nevertheless, some federal criminal statutes impose the same penalties for both the crimes they proscribe and for conspiracy to commit. Again, section 811, opts for a less sweeping approach than the Administration had proposed. It establishes equivalent sanctions for conspiracy and the underlying offense in cases of:

❗ arson committed within a federal enclave, 18 U.S.C. 81;
❗ killing committed while armed with a firearm in a federal building, 18 U.S.C. 930(c);
❗ destruction of communications facilities, 18 U.S.C. 1362;
❗ destruction of property within a federal enclave, 18 U.S.C. 1363;
❗ causing a train wreck, 18 U.S.C. 1922;
❗ providing material support to a terrorist, 18 U.S.C. 2339A;
❗ torture committed overseas under color of law, 18 U.S.C. 2340A;
❗ sabotage of a nuclear facility, 42 U.S.C. 2284;
❗ interfering with a flight crew within U.S. special aircraft jurisdiction, 49 U.S.C. 46504;
❗ carrying a weapon or explosive abroad an aircraft with U.S. special aircraft jurisdiction, 49 U.S.C. 46505; and
❗ sabotage of interstate gas pipeline facilities, 49 U.S.C. 60123.

Section 812. Post-Release Supervision of Terrorists.

When federal courts impose a sentence of a year or more upon a convicted defendant, they must also impose a term of supervised release, 18 U.S.C. 3583; U.S.S.G. §5D1.1. Supervised release is not unlike parole, except that it is ordinarily imposed in addition to rather than in lieu of a term, or portion of a term, of imprisonment. The term may be no longer than 5 years for most crimes and violations of the conditions of release may result in imprisonment for up to an additional 5 years, 18 U.S.C. 3583(e). There were proposals to create a maximum supervisory term of life for those convicted of acts of terrorism (subject to the calibrations of the Sentencing Commission). Section 812 amends section 3583 to provide for a supervisory release term of life or any term of years following conviction for a federal crime of terrorism as defined in 18 U.S.C. 2332b which resulted in death or involved a foreseeable risk of death or serious bodily injury, 18 U.S.C. 3583(j).

Section 813. Inclusion of Acts of Terrorism as Racketeering Activity.

Section 813 accepts the Administration's recommendation that all federal crimes of terrorism be included on the predicate offense list for RICO (racketeer influenced and corrupt organizations) which proscribes acquiring or operating, through the patterned commission of any of a series of predicate offenses, an enterprise whose activities affect interstate or foreign commerce, 18 U.S.C. 1961.

Section 814. Deterrence and Prevention of Cyberterrorism.

Computer fraud and abuse is a federal crime when it involves a federally protected computer, *i.e.*, a federal computer, a computer used by financial institutions, or a computer used in interstate or foreign commerce, 18 U.S.C. 1030. Section 814 increases the penalty for intentionally damaging a protected computer from imprisonment for not more than 5 years to imprisonment for not more than 10 years. It also raises the penalty for either intentionally or recklessly damaging a protected computer after having previously been convicted of computer abuse from imprisonment for not more than 10 years to imprisonment for not more than 20 years.

In order to trigger criminal or civil liability for causing damage to a federally protected computer, the damage must fall into one of several categories. It must involve losses of $5000 or more, or adversely affect certain medical data, or cause a physical injury, or threaten public health or safety. Section 814 supplies a fifth category – damage affecting a computer system used by or for the government for the administration of justice, national defense, or national security.

Section 814 supplies an explicit definition for the kinds of losses that may be considered in order to determine whether the $5000 threshold has been met. They consist of any reasonable cost including but not limited to those incurred to take corrective action, make damage assessments, and effect recuperation, as well as the consequential costs of interrupted service.

Section 815. Additional Defense to Civil Actions Relating to Preserving Records in Response to Government Requests.

Section 2707(e) of title 18 of the United States Code affords communications service providers with a good faith defense to civil or criminal liability for their cooperation in response to a warrant, subpoena or court order. Section 2703(f) requires them to return over records and other evidence at government request. Section 815 extends the good faith defense of section 2707(e) to cover civil and criminal liability for service provider cooperation with a request under section 2703(f).

Section 816. Development and Support of Cybersecurity Forensic Capabilities.

Section 816 authorizes annual appropriations of $50 million to establish regional computer forensic laboratories.

Section 817. Expansion of the Biological Weapons Statute.

Prior to enactment of the USA PATRIOT Act, federal law proscribed the use of biological agents or toxins as weapons, 18 U.S.C. 175. Section 817 supplements existing law with two federal crimes. First, it outlaws possession of a type or quantity of biological agents or toxins that cannot be justified for peaceful purposes, 18 U.S.C. 175(b). Second, consistent with federal prohibitions on the possession of firearms, 18 U.S.C. 922(g), and explosives, 18 U.S.C. 842(i), it makes it a federal offense for certain individuals – convicted felons, illegal aliens, and fugitives and the like – to possess biological toxins or agents, 18 U.S.C. 175b. Both offenses are punishable by imprisonment for not more than ten years and/or a fine of not more than $250,000.

Title IX – Improved Intelligence

Section 901. Responsibilities of Director of Central Intelligence Regarding Foreign Intelligence Collected Under Foreign Intelligence Surveillance Act of 1978.

Only the President or the Attorney General may authorize application for a FISA surveillance or physical search order, 50 U.S.C. 1802, 1804, 1822, 1823. Information acquired by means of a FISA order may be shared with other federal officials, including members of the intelligence community, as long as minimization procedures are observed, 50 U.S.C. 1806, 1825. FISA minimization procedures are crafted "consistent with the need of the United States to obtain, produce, and disseminate foreign intelligence information," 50 U.S.C. 1801(h), 1821(4).

Section 901 amends the National Security Act of 1947, 50 U.S.C. 403-3(c), instructing the Director of the Central Intelligence[12] to establish priorities and requirements concerning the use of the Foreign Intelligence Surveillance Act (FISA) and to assist the Attorney General to ensure that information generated by the

---

[12] The Director of Central Intelligence is simultaneously Director of the Central Intelligence Agency (CIA), the President's principal advisor on national security intelligence matters, and coordinating head of the intelligence community, 50 U.S.C. 403(a).

execution of FISA surveillance and physical search orders is disseminated so as to be used efficiently and effectively for foreign intelligence purposes. The intelligence community, however, must work through the good offices of the Attorney General to use FISA orders in the performance of its responsibilities, since in the absence of specific statutory or executive order authority, the Director is not permitted to direct, manage, or undertake execution of a FISA order.

Section 902. Inclusion of International Terrorist Activities Within the Scope of Foreign Intelligence Under the National Security Act of 1947.

Section 3 of the National Security Act defines the kind of information that constitutes "foreign intelligence" for purposes of the Act, 50 U.S.C. 5401a(2). Section 902 adds information relating to the activities of international terrorists to the definition.

Section 903. Sense of Congress on the Establishment and Maintenance of Intelligence Relationships to Acquire Information on Terrorists and Terrorist Organizations.

Section 903 expresses the sense of Congress that members of the intelligence community should be outgoing in their efforts to acquire information about terrorists and terrorist organizations.

Section 904. Temporary Authority to Defer Submittal to Congress of Reports on Intelligence and Intelligence-Related Matters.

Section 904 permits intelligence community agencies to defer submission of required intelligence reports to Congress (other than the reports on covert actions required under 50 U.S.C. 413a, 413b) until February 1, 2002. They may delay submission further, if compliance would impede counterintelligence activities.

Section 905. Disclosure to Director of Central Intelligence of Foreign Intelligence-Related Information With Respect to Criminal Investigations.

The Attorney General in consultation with the Director of Central Intelligence has been directed in section 905 to develop guidelines to ensure the dissemination to the intelligence community of foreign intelligence information unearthed during the course of a criminal investigation. The guidelines may embody exceptions necessary to prevent jeopardizing an ongoing criminal investigation or other significant law enforcement interests. They should contain a means for reporting back to the intelligence community on the action taken or to be taken on the basis of information which elements of the intelligence community have passed to the Justice Department.

Section 906. Foreign Terrorist Asset Tracking Center.

Following the attacks of September 11, the Treasury Department announced the creation of an inter-agency foreign terrorist asset tracking center, which reportedly consists of agents from the Customs Service, Office of Foreign Asset Control (OFAC), Internal Revenue Service, FBI, and CIA.

Section 906 asks for a joint report from the Secretary of the Treasury, the Attorney General, and the Director of Central Intelligence on the feasibility of reconfiguring the Center and OFAC into an entity able to analyze the financial capabilities and resources of international terrorists organizations, on the extent to which the Financial Crimes Enforcement Center (FinCEN) should be included, and on a legislative proposal detailing the specifics of any such entity found whose creation they find feasible and desirable.

Section 907. National Virtual Translation Center.

Section 907 instructs the Director of Central Intelligence, in consultation with the Director of the FBI to report on the establishment of a national virtual translation center for the purpose providing timely and accurate translations of foreign intelligence.

Section 908. Training of Government Officials Regarding Identification and Use of Foreign Intelligence.

Section 908 authorizes the necessary appropriations to train federal officials who do not ordinarily deal with foreign intelligence matters and state and local government officials who may encounter foreign intelligence in the course of a terrorist attack. The training would assist the officials to identify and use foreign intelligence information in the performance of their duties.

Title X – Miscellaneous

Section 1001. Review of the Department of Justice.

As the House Judiciary Committee, from which this proposal first emerged, explained, "In the wake of several significant incidents of security lapses and breach of regulations, there has arisen the need for independent oversight of the Federal Bureau of Investigation. Oversight of the Federal Bureau of Investigation is currently under the jurisdiction of the Department of Justice Office of Professional Responsibility. This section directs the Inspector General of the Department of Justice to appoint a Deputy Inspector General for Civil Rights, Civil Liberties, and the Federal Bureau of Investigation who shall be responsible for supervising independent oversight of the FBI until September 30, 2004. This section also directs the Deputy Inspector to review all information alleging abuses of civil rights, civil liberties, and racial and ethnic profiling by employees of the Department of Justice, which could include allegations of inappropriate profiling at the border," H.Rept. 107-236, at 78. (2001).

Section 1002. Sense of Congress.

Section 1002 expresses the sense of Congress that the rights of all Americans include those of Sikh-Americans should be protected in the quest to apprehend those responsible for the attacks of September 11; that violence or discrimination against any Americans including Sikh-Americans should be condemned; law enforcement authorities should work to prevent all Americans including Sikh-Americans from becoming crime victims; and that federal authorities should prosecute those responsible to the fullest extent of the law.

Section 1003. Definition of "Electronic Surveillance".

The Foreign Intelligence Surveillance Act (FISA) allows federal authorities to conduct "electronic surveillance" under certain limited foreign intelligence gathering purposes. Section 217 allows federal law enforcement officers to intercept the communications of computer trespassers within the system in which they are intruders, 18 U.S.C. 2511(2)(i). Section 1003 amends FISA to make it clear that the computer trespasser exception does not apply to FISA surveillance orders. FISA surveillance orders may be issued to acquire the communications of a computer trespasser, 50 U.S.C. 1801(f)(2).

Section 1004. Venue in Money Laundering Cases.

The Constitution provides that, the "Trial of all Crimes . . . shall be held in the State where the said Crimes shall have been committed; but when not committed within any State, the Trial shall be at such Place or Places as the Congress may by Law have directed," *U.S.Const.* Art.III, §2, 3, and that "[i]n all criminal prosecutions, the accused shall enjoy the right to a speedy and public trial, by an impartial jury of the State and district wherein the crime shall have been committed, which district shall have been previously ascertained by law," *U.S.Const.* Amend. VI. When a crime begins in one district and continues on to another, trial may be constitutionally held in either district, *United States v. Anderson*, 328 U.S. 699, 704-5 (1946). Thus, the federal crime of conspiracy, which consists of the agreement to commit a federal crime plus an overt act committed in furtherance of the conspiracy, may be tried wherever the agreement occurred or wherever an overt act in its furtherance was committed, *Hyde v. United States*, 225 U.S. 347, 363 (1912).

This doctrine of continuing offenses, however, is not boundless. In *United States v. Cabrales*, 524 U.S. 1 (1998), a unanimous Supreme Court held that a charge of laundering of the proceeds of a Missouri drug trafficking operation in Florida could not tried in Missouri. In the course of its opinion, the Court observed, that "[m]oney laundering. . . arguably might rank as a continuing offense, triable in more that one place, if the launderer acquired the funds in one district and transported them into another," 524 U.S. at 8.

Section 1004 relies on this language when it permits a prosecution for money laundering in violation of either 18 U.S.C. 1956 or 1957 in the place where the predicate offense occurred "if the defendant participated in the transfer of the proceeds" of the predicate offense from the district in which the predicate offense occurred into the district in which the laundering occurred, 18 U.S.C. 1956(i)(1). The section also permits prosecution where an overt act in furtherance of conspiracy to violation the money laundering sections occurs, 18 U.S.C. 1956(i)(2).

Section 1005. First Responders Assistance Act.

Section 1005 authorizes appropriations of $25 million for each fiscal year from 2003 through 2007 to permit the Attorney General to make grants to state and local governments for terrorism prevention and antiterrorism training of fire fighters and other first responders. Each state from which a qualified grant application is submitted is entitled to no less than 0.5% of the total amount appropriated under section 1005 for that year.

Section 1006. Inadmissibility of Aliens Engaged in Money Laundering.

Section 1006 makes aliens who have participated in money laundering inadmissible for admission into the United States. The Secretary of State is instructed to maintain a watchlist to be consulted to ensure that aliens involved in money laundering are not allowed to enter this country.

Section 1007. Authorization of Funds for DEA Police Training in South and Central Asia.

The Taliban and al Qaeda reportedly fund their activities in part by trafficking in heroin. The material used to process the heroin flow into Afghanistan from South and Central Asia and the processed heroin is transported into world commerce through Turkey. Section 1007 authorizes appropriations of $5 million for Drug Enforcement Administration training for the police of Turkey and of the countries of South and Central Asia in order to disrupt heroin production in Afghanistan.

Section 1008. Feasibility Study on Use of Biometric Identifier Scanning System With Access to the FBI Integrated Automated Fingerprint Identification System at Overseas Consular Posts and Points of Entry to the United States.

"Section 1008 requires the Attorney General to conduct a study of the feasibility of utilizing a biometric identifier (fingerprint) scanning system at consular offices and points of entry into the United States to identify aliens who may be wanted in connection with criminal or terrorist investigations in the United States or abroad. A biometric fingerprint scanning system is a sophisticated computer scanning technology that analyzes a person's fingerprint and compares the measurement with a verified sample digitally stored in the system. The accuracy of these systems is claimed to be above 99.9%. The biometric identifier system contemplated by this section would have access to the database of the Federal Bureau of Investigation Integrated Automated Fingerprint Identification System. The section requires that the Attorney General shall submit a summary of the findings of the study to Congress within 90 days.

Section 1009. Study of Access.

Section 1009 authorizes $250,000 for the Federal Bureau of Investigation to study the feasibility of providing airlines with computer access to the names of those the federal government suspects of terrorism.

Section 1010. Temporary Authority to Contract With Local and State Governments for Performance of Security Functions at United States Military Installations.

Subject to limited exceptions, the Department of Defense may not contract for fire fighting or security-guard functions to be performed on military installations, 10

U.S.C. 2465. Section 1010 creates another exception and allows neighboring state and local authorities to perform security functions for military installations and facilities pursuant to contracts with the Defense Department for a period up to 180 days after the completion of Operation Enduring Freedom.

Section 1011. Crimes Against Charitable Americans.

The Telemarketing and Consumer Fraud and Abuse Prevention Act, 15 U.S.C. 6101 *et seq.* empowers the Federal Trade Commission (FTC) to promulgate regulations to prevent telemarketing deception. It is a federal crime to impersonate members or agents of the Red Cross for fraudulent purposes, 18 U.S.C. 917. And the federal criminal code imposes special penalties for telemarketing fraud, 18 U.S.C. 2325-2327.

Section 1011 brings telephone charitable solicitations under the FTC's regulatory umbrella, 15 U.S.C. 6102, 6106. It increases the penalty for impersonating Red Cross members or agents in order make fraudulent charitable solicitations from imprisonment for not more than 1 year to imprisonment for not more than 5 years, 18 U.S.C. 917. It also amends 18 U.S.C. 2325 in order make the enhanced telemarketing fraud penalties applicable to fraudulent charitable telephone solicitations, 18 U.S.C. 2325.

Section 1012. Limitation on Issuance of Hazmat Licenses.

The Secretary of Transportation exercises regulatory authority over the safe interstate transportation of hazardous materials (hazmat), 49 U.S.C. 5101 *et seq.*, and over commercial motor vehicle operators, 49 U.S.C. 31301 *et seq.* Section 1012 enacts 49 U.S.C. 5103a, which limits the issuance of hazmat licenses to instances where the Secretary of Transportation has certified that the applicant is not a security risk. It allows the states to request a background check from the Attorney General for a criminal record, for illegal alien status, and with Interpol. It expands the definition of hazardous materials to include chemical and biological materials and agents, and authorizes the Secretary of the Transportation to require the states to report relevant related information. Section 1012 also amends 49 U.S.C. 31305 with respect to the minimum standards for commercial motor vehicle operator fitness to include a determination that the applicant has been determined under section 5103a not to pose a security risk.

Section 1013. Expressing the Sense of the Senate Concerning the Provision of Funding for Bioterrorism Preparedness and Response.

Section 1013 expresses the sense of the Senate that there should be an expanded level of public expenditures to prepare and respond to threats of bioterrorism.

Section 1014. Grant Program for State and Local Domestic Preparedness Support.

Section 1014 authorizes appropriations in whatever sums are necessary for fiscal years 2002 through 2007 to make OJP grants to the state and local units of government to enhance their capacity to respond to terrorist attacks including those involving use of weapons of mass destruction, biological, chemical, nuclear, radiological, incendiary, chemical and explosive devises. The grants may be used to train and equip first responders. The Department of Justice may use no more than 3% of the appropriations for salaries and administrative expenses and each state is entitled to not less than 0.75% of the amount appropriated in any given fiscal year (not less than 0.25% for each of Guam, the Virgin Islands, American Samoa and the Northern Mariana Islands).

Section 1015. Expansion and Reauthorization of the Crime Identification Technology Act for Antiterrorism Grants to States and Localities.

The Crime Identification Technology Act, Public Law 105-251, 112 Stat. 1871 (1998), 42 U.S.C. 14601, authorizes the OJP to issue state and local grants for the development of various integrated information and identification systems and for that purpose authorizes appropriations of $250 million for each fiscal year through 2003. Section 1015 amends section 14601 to permit grants for related terrorism purposes and extends the authorization of appropriations in the amount of $250 million per year through fiscal year 2007.

Section 1016. Critical Infrastructures Protection.

Section 1016 authorizes appropriations of $20 million for fiscal year 2002 to be used by the Department of Defense's Defense Threat Reduction Agency for activities of National Infrastructure Simulation and Analysis Center.